Christ in the
Early Christian Hymns

Christ in the
Early Christian Hymns

Daniel Liderbach

PAULIST PRESS
New York / Mahwah, N.J.

Acknowledgements

The Publisher gratefully acknowledges use of the following materials:
English translations of "Ales Dei Nuntius," "Quicumque Christum Quaeri-tis," "Salvete Flores Martyrum," "Audit Tyrannus Anxius" and "O Sola Mag-narum Urbium" from *The Hymns of the Breviary and Missal,* edited by Dom Matthew Britt, O.S.B., copyright © 1948, Benziger Brothers, New York. Used by permission of Benziger Publishing Company.

Scripture quotations are from the Revised Standard Version of the Bible, copyright © 1946, 1952, 1971 by the Division of Christian Education of the National Council of the Churches of Christ in the U.S.A. Used by permission.

Cover design by Nick Markell

Library of Congress Cataloging-in-Publication Data

Liderbach, Daniel,   1941–
    Christ in the early Christian hymns / by Daniel Liderbach.
        p.   cm.
    Includes bibliographical references and index.
    ISBN 0-8091-3809-3 (alk. paper)
    1. Jesus Christ—Natures—History of doctrines—Early church, ca. 30–600.
2. Hymns, Early Christian—History and criticism. I. Title.
BT212.L53   1998
232′.09′015—dc21   98-28762
                                                                          CIP

Published by Paulist Press
997 Macarthur Boulevard
Mahwah, New Jersey 07430

www.paulistpress.com

Printed and bound in the
United States of America

Contents

This book is dedicated
to
Brian, Susan, Kathleen, Mary,
Sharon, Mark, and John,
my brothers and sisters,
the soil that supports me
and the atmosphere that nurtures me.

Preface

This project was carried out with the assistance of several people whom I want to acknowledge. Lawrence Boadt, my editor at Paulist Press, helped me to sculpt the text. The Society of Jesus made time available to me and provided me with the research tools needed for this work, and for that I express gratitude. Daniel P. Jamros, a specialist in the works of Georg F. W. Hegel, read and critiqued my use of Hegel's synthetic dialectic. And finally, Jean Campbell kindly proofread the manuscript and assisted me with the index.

I. Christology in Worship

The church has generally identified Christ Jesus with a Christology *from above;* namely, an interpretation of Christ that emerges from humans' reflection upon their belief in the divine Christ Jesus.

However Christology *from below* occurs when people reflect on the basis of their experience upon their awareness of the identity of the human Jesus. In this study I have focused upon the awareness the earliest Christian communities expressed in their hymns of worship. These hymns convey the communities' beliefs or trust in the God of Jesus Christ. The hymn form captured the community's effort to express its belief in Jesus with an understanding represented not only by a rational dialogue, but by an imaginative one as well.

This study will focus upon the latter of these approaches, that is, Christology from below, or the human awareness of the identity of Christ Jesus as experientially based.

The point of departure, as well as the constant reference point throughout this study, is the Spirit that is present within and directs not only the centralized church authorities, but the worshiping community as well. "The worshiping community" is the gathering of those who had come forth to an accustomed place for worship according to a regular schedule for prayer. That community presumably had leaders who were not only members of the local community, but also charismatically gifted spokesmen for the attitudes of the community.

The Spirit guides the community by articulating a response to the Spirit in communal worship. The use of hymns reflects the community's interaction both with its social and cultural environments, with its imaginative belief and its reason, and with the Spirit in its midst vis-à-vis its sense perceptions.

The teaching church, however, needs to direct more official self-expression from an awareness of the social and cultural events within the environment and from that of a respect for the spontaneous response to the Spirit by the community. The church also directs official self-expression in worship from the perspective of accepted doctrine that has been passed down from prior divine inspiration. There is therefore an unexpressed dialectic between the more authoritative teaching of the church and the spontaneous responses of the imagined belief of the community of believers.

This study assumes that the worshiping community reveals its reactions to changes within the social and cultural environment of the community; that self-expression is revealed in hymns. Moreover the hymns disclose the Spirit's guidance in the felt experience of the community.

Thus, for example, if a community continues to worship in a specific location, it does so because of its response to both material and spiritual forces within the environment. If it continues to use certain hymns in its worship, it does so because of material and spiritual forces within the environment. Similarly if it ceases to use other hymns, then it does so because of its spontaneous response to those same forces.

The worshiping community therefore does not perceive itself as having the authority to act with the same sense of independence and autonomy that a strictly rational community may perceive itself to be able to exercise. Rather this community responds with a spontaneous awareness of the different forces—relative to the directives of the Spirit—that influence it.

We can also assume that when a group of people is responsive to the flow of events in its environment—one must recall that some of those events are spiritual—the group is being responsive to the Spirit who moves within the environment. The community's self-expressions within that environment, such as its use of hymns, will reveal the attitude of belief of the community.

Church authorities, such as bishops, may reveal attitudes that are at times responses to the culture of the environment. Higher ecclesiastical authorities may also reveal attitudes that are acultural. They have insisted, for example, upon a doctrine of human morality, which forces within the environment seem to reject.

This study focuses upon the hymns used by the whole worshiping community; these express the community's self-awareness as it responds to its environment. Moreover this study assumes that the community therefore can be more responsive to the Spirit who moves in the environment, an authority that must at times express itself as relatively independent of the environment. Thus this study also addresses the Spirit as its subject matter because of the conviction that the Spirit is active within the community's self-expression of its response to the social and cultural environment. Moreover, active in the environment, the Spirit has directed the community to express a Spirit-inspired faith in its hymns.

1. First, the early hymns are considered. These reveal a Christology that identifies Christ Jesus as Savior, as Redeemer, as the Son of God, and as the model for humanity. One of the oldest and most important beliefs of the early Christians was that God had exalted Christ to the right hand of God, that is,

to a status of Lord, as a reward for his having been the model for the human response to God.[1]

That very early Christian belief, which is known as "adoptionism," confessed that the Christ had preexisted his birth, had emptied himself in order to become a man, and had then returned to be with the God from whom he had come. That "adoptionism" is articulated in several New Testament texts, for example, the Petrine speeches in Acts (Acts 2-10), the Synoptic accounts of the baptism of Jesus (Mk 1:9-11; Mt 3:13-17; Lk 3:21-22), the prologue of John's gospel (Jn 1:1-18), and the letters by Paul to the Romans (1:4) and the Philippians (2:9-11).

The prominence of this belief in the Jewish Christianity of the second and third centuries has been abundantly documented, for example, by the historical work of Jean Danielou. However those early Jewish Christians had not identified Jesus as God.

Moreover the hymns that represent such adoptionism, such as Hebrews 1:3, Philippians 2:9-11, and John's Prologue, not only manifest this early Christian belief, but also reveal the Spirit's guidance of the community according to the principle that we will see below, the "Rule of Faith."[2] The goal of this study is to articulate the form of belief that the Spirit had influenced the early community to express in its acts of worship.

The meaning of the guidance of the community by the Spirit needs to be addressed. Within a community there are certain attitudes that are shared. Some members have the charism to articulate these attitudes of the community, of which other members have only a vague awareness. Thus, for example, a member of the community might articulate intolerance for a business operating within the community. Prior to that articulation the community might have had no more than a dim awareness of its intolerance for that business. However, after the member's articulation, the community recognizes that it has been led by the Spirit to acknowledge a communal intolerance.

Those who are familiar with the New Testament might well recall at this point the report in the Acts of the Apostles of the decision of the Jewish Christians, who had gathered to discuss and to articulate a communal attitude about Gentile converts, that "It is the decision of the Holy Spirit and of us not to place on you any burden beyond these necessities..." (Acts 15:28). That early gathering of Jewish Christians had recognized in its communal decision the guidance that the Holy Spirit had given them within their midst.

So in any Christian community the Holy Spirit is believed to be present and to be guiding the community within its communally articulated attitudes and judgments.

Along with adoptionism there was another widespread belief in the earliest community. Jewish Christians, as Paul (Phil 2:9-11) and John (1:1-18) had expressed, believed that Christ had descended from God and then had ascended to be with God.[3] This persisted until at least the third century.

2. Then Arius and his doctrine emerged within the Christian community and spread widely. Arius taught a logical inference drawn from an article of the creed (which would be explicitly formed at Nicaea); namely, that Christ was "begotten from the Father before all ages." He also drew his inference from the Christology that the believing community had been expressing in its hymns since the beginning, that Christ Jesus was the Savior, the Redeemer, the Son of God and the model for humanity, but not univocally God.

3. After the condemnation of Arius (325 C.E.), a new genre of ideologically purified Christian hymns appeared. They manifest a Christology which insisted that the identity of Christ Jesus is of the same substance as the Father. That Christology, however, was ideologically imposed upon the Christian community by the Council of Nicaea (325 C.E.); it is not explicitly found in the hymns that the community had been using

prior to the formulation of the doctrine by the Council of
Nicaea.

Thus that Christology needs a category separate from
the earlier responses of the community to the Spirit in the cultural environment. The shift to the Nicaean Christology is evident in hymns that appeared after 325. They express an
anti-Arian polemical source, which is previously unknown in
the hymns used by the Christian community.

4. The hymns following the Arian years manifest an
evolved and more cautious Christology—they carefully insist
upon the identity of Christ as being of the same substance as
the Father, that is, they insist that Christ is God's own self.
The community would continue to confess that approach to
Christ's relationship with the Father until the Council of
Chalcedon (451 C.E.).

After the Council of Chalcedon, the hymns again
returned to the identification of Christ as a dialectical tension
between Christ as divine and Christ as human, between the
imagination of faith and the empiricism of experience.

Among those later hymns are some that appear to be
more spontaneous and thus presumably more responsive to
the Spirit; others are more cautious and thus theological.

For example, among the anonymous Ambrosian hymns
are some that appear to be more spontaneous and thus more
representative of the belief of the people. They have no known
authors. Perhaps they were used in worship because they represented the belief that nameless members of the community
recognized as their own.

Among those same hymns are others that are more cautious and theological. There are also hymns actually composed by Ambrose himself; they were his efforts to defend a
belief that the church had imposed upon the community.

However it may not be clear to the critical believer that
early Christian hymns manifest the guidance of the Spirit, as
this study will argue. Hymns may rather express the guidance

of bishops, who perhaps had wisely used hymns in order to form the belief of the community. Therefore the following chapters will explore the degree to which the belief of the community determined not only the hymns, but also the hymns' doctrine of Christ's identity. The community's belief is articulated in the "Rule of Faith." The task of the following chapters is to discern to what degree the Rule of Faith directed the identity of Christ Jesus formulated at the Council of Chalcedon.

II. The Significance of Hymns: The Rule of Faith

The problem, often ignored, in the doctrine of Christ Jesus is that the official church has identified Christ neither as the God nor as a human, but as both simultaneously. If we were to identify anything within our experience as having simultaneously the identity both of one substance and of another, we would be speaking foolishness. Thus, we would not point to an object and identify it as both a tree and a dog. Nonetheless the church has been quite careful so to identify Christ Jesus: he is fully divine and fully human simultaneously. That doctrine envisioned the foci with which believers are to comprehend the identity of Christ. However those foci—the human and divine identities of Christ—are not intended to be understood as only theoretical. On the contrary, the Council of Chalcedon evidently intended to acknowledge that the identity of Jesus of Nazareth remains incomprehensible; nonetheless the Council insisted that the community believe Christ indeed has not only theoretically, but also actually, two natures—divine and human—in the one hypostasis, Jesus of Nazareth.

In order to discuss this problem, one might wisely situate it within its proper context. The context in which to situate the identity of Christ Jesus is the functioning of the Rule of Faith.

The Belief of the Community Determines the Doctrine of the Church.

The Rule of Faith refers to the church's ancient criterion that the Spirit indicates genuine doctrine by directing the faithful community to believe as doctrine what it expresses in its worship.

Belief signifies for the church the trust that the community acknowledges in its commitment to the God with whom it forms its covenant or its relationship.

Doctrine signifies the teaching that the church fashions as articles to which the community of believers is challenged to acknowledge as the intellectual confession of its covenant.

As early as the fifth century Pope Celestine had expressed the Rule: *"...legem credendi lex statuat supplicandi,"* that is, the rule of faith determines the rule of doctrine.[1] Alternately expressed, the Rule of Faith acknowledges, belief reveals doctrine. The ancient tradition of the church has passed on such a reverence for the autonomy of the community's belief. Traditionally doctrine has not determined belief; rather belief has determined doctrine.

Such a rule appears to focus upon an orientation different from the orientation that the church might appear to follow. One might be tempted to assume that the Rule of Faith is more ignored than observed. However one who studiously examines whether the Spirit directs doctrine from within the experience of faith, that is, who examines how doctrines have been determined, discovers that the church has quite faithfully observed the Rule of Faith. Doctrine has developed and develops still as the Spirit has directed and continues to direct the community spontaneously to believe.

Nevertheless in defining some doctrines the church seem to have ignored the Rule of Faith, such as in the doctrine of papal infallibility. Nonetheless the centralized church has with very few exceptions attempted first to be sensitive to the guidance of the Spirit within the community and only later to propose doctrine.

Many Church Doctrines Resulted from the Faith of the Community.

From its early years the church has formed its doctrine so that it reflected the belief that had been expressed by the community of the faithful.

The more ancient Christian doctrines were so formulated. For example, such doctrines as: Christ Jesus is God and man, Mary as mother of Christ was a virgin, Mary is the mother of God, and the one God is three are doctrines fashioned according to the belief of the community. The belief confessed by the members of the church has been received from the source that many call *tradition,* but that others, including this author, name as the Spirit.

Since *tradition* is the more commonly used term, reflection might begin there. Tradition has been passed on to the members of the church by means of a range of affirmations that includes catechetical teaching, homiletic explanations, precise doctrine or definitions, and the hymns used in worship. Not only the hymns, but also the other forms of affirmations have been passed on to the members of the church within the community's experience of worship.[2]

The tradition that had been passed on had been formulated by the church's having consulted a series of criteria for the identification of doctrine. One such criterion was the testimony of scripture. Another was the tradition of the church's teaching, some of which antedate the composition of the scriptures. For example, in 1 Corinthians 15:3–8, which is the earliest passage in the New Testament, Paul refers to a tradition that antedates this earliest New Testament writing: "I delivered to you what I also received, that Christ died for our sins in accordance with the scriptures...."

On the other hand, many of those who consider themselves to be more orthodox in belief use as their standard for faith not tradition, but either the word of scripture or the official dogma of the church. Those criteria can be the final standard of appeal concerning any question about belief for the more orthodox.

Many church historians prefer to consider social dynamics that fashioned culture as the final standard of appeal concerning the origin of doctrine. For example, the data about fourth-and fifth-century European self-consciousness make it evident that there was then a dialectical relationship between church doctrine and imperial norms for maintaining civil order in the governments' courts in both Rome and Constantinople. The emperors at Rome and Constantinople in the fourth and fifth centuries, in order to establish civic order within the empire, ordered the church to settle the question about the identity of Jesus. The emperor in Constantinople, the pious old soldier, Marcian, had therefore summoned and had intended to direct the Council of Chalcedon to fashion a doctrine of Christ according to his own belief. From such data the historian might conclude that those emperors, who reigned in the fourth-and fifth-century culture, had been the forces that fashioned the doctrine of the church concerning Jesus Christ's identity.

Theological Reflection upon the Rule of Faith

Yet, theology might be more concerned with other criteria for the determining of doctrine. Irenaeus of Lyons (c. 130-c. 200), one of the first great Christian theologians, insisted that the church's doctrine was to be determined not by such regional politics, nor even by scripture, nor by ecclesiastical decree, but by the tradition of doctrine that had been passed on within the official church. Thus he derived from tradition the doctrine that all were to confess. From the traditional dogmas of the community he formulated a statement of faith, that is, a creed.[3] Irenaeus had thus acknowledged that the church was to fashion its doctrine not by consulting texts of scripture, nor by weighing the value of theologians' writings, but by sensitively retaining those doctrines that the community had retained as valid, by repeating the doctrines of tradition.

Similarly Origen, Ignatius, Aristides, Justin Martyr, Tertullian, and Hippolytus had each distilled from the community's traditions of belief those teachings that they considered to be authoritative and thus valid for all the faithful.

The content of such universal faith may indeed have been quite modest, judging from such quotations as: "There is one God....Jesus Christ is Lord....It is also necessary to believe in the Holy Spirit."[4] Nonetheless, the important issue for this book is not the content of the derived statement of faith, but rather the method by which that doctrine was formulated. Irenaeus's method of formulating doctrine had been to gather those creedal assertions that the church had maintained as the tradition of the community, that is, those assertions that the Holy Spirit had revealed within the community to be the content of the church's belief.

Irenaeus's criterion for formulating doctrine manifests his endorsement of the Rule of Faith, in other words, that doctrine emerges from the belief of the community.

Thus, because of the growth of belief within the community, the church in the fourth century had put aside its prior ambiguity about the virginity of Mary and acknowledged the doctrine of her virginity, which Athanasius of Alexandria had discerned and formulated in his *Letter to Virgins*.[5]

Prosper of Aquitaine (c. 390–c. 463) in his *The Call of All Nations* formulated the Rule of Faith: doctrine was to be fashioned in such a manner that it imitates the prayer which is practiced by all priests and all faithful throughout the world.

"Prayer" signifies the articulation of trust in the God with whom the community of believers is interrelating. Since prayer is the articulation of trust in God, the expression of that trust reveals the belief of the church community in the God with whom it is interrelating. Thus, doctrine based upon prayer expressed what the community genuinely believed. Therefore the teachers within the entire church needed (and need) to be concerned with the way all believers pray—concerned that the church teach those doctrines which emerge from the light with which the Spirit illumines the church communities.

Prosper of Aquitaine's intention had been that the church discern whether doctrine emerged from the belief of the wider community so as to elude the plague of faddish belief and preserve traditional belief.[6] Nevertheless, Prosper recognized there would have to be considerable effort expended in order for the church to discern the belief that comes into focus within the prayer of the community.

In the fourth century there was a shift in the belief of the community. The community had begun to pray to Christ the Lord as if to God. As a result of that shift the church was wise enough to recognize a need to formulate church doctrine: that Christ the Lord is God together with God the Father.[7]

The Rule of Faith Used by the Council of Nicaea

In order to address that change in the belief of the community, the church convened the Council of Nicaea in 325. Although there were a variety of issues that the Council was to address, the major issue before the fathers assembled there was to derive a new doctrine from the development of the faithful believers' experience in prayer regarding Christ. The church thus directed the fathers who assembled at the Council of

Nicaea to allow the experience of the community to direct them to a new doctrine about Christ Jesus.

However the "Rule of Faith" followed by the Council of Nicaea was entirely distinct from that which Irenaeus, who lived more than a hundred years earlier, had articulated as the one rule of faith.

Irenaeus had basically formulated a creed by identifying the commonly held doctrines. Irenaeus composed a set of dogmas that he considered to be binding upon all members of the community.[8]

However, the Rule of Faith that the fathers at the Council of Nicaea were to discover was not a discernment of the established dogma or creed of tradition, but a discernment of the beliefs of the community. Communal beliefs were to determine the current doctrine.

Doctrine was derived from the prayer of the believing community; prayer was thus used in the fourth century as the methodological criterion by which the doctrine about Christ Jesus was to be formulated. The norm for that new doctrine had not especially been the word of scripture, nor solely the official church's traditional content of faith. Rather, that norm was the belief of the community insofar as that belief could be identified.

Many of the foundational beliefs of those who believed in the God of Jesus Christ in the fourth century had been fashioned much earlier, between the death of Jesus around 30 C.E. and the beginning of the New Testament in the early 50s. Prior to the writing of the New Testament documents, there had been no official, written word nor authoritative, communal tradition of teaching from which to derive doctrine. However there had been a communal awareness of prayer and worship. From that awareness the foundational doctrines had been fashioned. Some of those doctrines had been passed down to the community of the church in the fourth century. Believers were generally conscious that the continuing tradition summoned them to remain faithful adherents to the worldview of the tradition.

Yet the community of the fourth century was also summoned to be faithful to the worldview that had been forming within its own era. That perspective was that which the Council of Nicaea was to express as doctrine.

A century and a quarter after Nicaea, that method of deriving doctrine from the community's belief as expressed in prayer was again to be used to derive the definition of Christ at the Council of Chalcedon (451 C.E.).

Faith—Definition of Christ as an Enigma

The critically reflective individual might indeed respond critically that the Council of Chalcedon's definition of Christ as human and divine is a challenge the human intellect cannot meet. The intelligent believer cannot but ask how Jesus, who was a human individual within a specific historical era, could have been identified as not only a historical human, but also as divine.

Certainly the Christians in the eighteenth-century Age of Enlightenment would have been conditioned to halt at the church's acknowledgment of the two natures of Christ that the Council had derived from the Rule of Faith. Because the Enlightenment insisted that everything, including Christian doctrine, was to be interpreted rationally, a rational eighteenth-century Christian would have paused in confusion at the church's challenge that one was to accept that some sort of a divine trust had been bestowed upon the fathers of the Council. As a result the Council of Chalcedon required the individual to interpret church doctrine not in terms of reason, but in terms of the Spirit's guidance, which the fathers had supposedly discerned within the beliefs of the community.[9]

Even more, Christians in the twentieth-century's postmodernist era have been conditioned by their era's skepticism similarly to halt at the definition that Christ has two natures.

The skeptical individual seeks for a foundation that grounds Chalcedon's extraordinary judgment about Jesus' identity.

Theology's appeal to the Rule of Faith as the criterion of judgment might provide some modest validity for the definition of Jesus as human and divine. Thus, if theology is to be attentive to the culture in which the individual believers in the church live, then she might prudently direct the probing believer to such a criterion.

To the degree that the skeptical postmodernist believer discovers that the church used the criterion of the Rule of Faith to formulate the definition of Christ's identity, one might then be able to discover not a rational criterion, but an arational, elusive criterion, which was in the public expression of fifth-century believers' faith. Their public prayer provides an adequate basis upon the arational, through which a skeptical believer might discover the communities' arational confession of a doctrine of the identity of Christ.

The postmodern, pragmatic believer might be able to assent to the validity of using only the faith of the community as the criterion of doctrine. Scripture alone might appear to the informed skeptic to be too much the product of mythmakers; the same skepticism might consider the orthodox tradition of the church to have been an unreflective inheritance of political precedent. Certainly the cultural and political dynamics of the fifth-century Roman and Byzantine empires do not appear to satisfy the postrational believer's search for a pragmatic basis for belief. Such cultural or political dynamics may have been little more than passionate, ideological debates in the marketplaces. Yet the believer might conclude that all of those influences together might have led the community to a belief in Jesus' identity.

An individual of the twentieth century might believe, however vaguely, in the presence of God active within the world and therefore might accept that the Spirit of God, acting through the several dynamics of fifth-century culture, led the community of believers to the faith in Jesus that became doctrine at the Council of Chalcedon.

The Rule of Faith Used by the Early Church

The Rule of Faith as the method of determining doctrine was acknowledged very early in the history of the Christian community not only by the official church, but also by very early Christian theologians such as Irenaeus, Origen, and Prosper of Aquitaine. Even the unorthodox theologians Cerdo and Marcion, whose teachings flourished in the church in the middle of the second century, recognized that the church needed to formulate its doctrine in harmony with the experience of the believing community.

The precise belief of the community that Cerdo and Marcion discerned within the experience of the community was that the community believed in opposing deities, one good and one evil. Though the church had decided to reject their doctrine, the two were yet another representation of the validity of the Rule of Faith; they had formulated their doctrine from the beliefs that they had discerned within the community of believers.[10]

While today there may be many who casually dismiss Cerdo's and Marcion's doctrine of two opposing deities as foolish, the serious student recognizes that Cerdo and Marcion admitted in the second century that there was validity in looking to the communal expression of belief in order to discern doctrine. They therefore risked formulating the doctrine of the dualism of deities, which was contrary to the traditional doctrine of the church. The question for them, as for any theologians who take the Rule of Faith seriously, is not whether the newly formulated doctrine is in harmony with traditional doctrines, but whether it expresses the faith of the community.

In any age the faith of the community will not be uniform—there have always been differences. Indeed the faith of a community in one locality might conflict with the faith of a community in another locality. Nonetheless, if the church hopes to observe the Rule of Faith, then it needs to take the means to identify belief that is generally endorsed by those who seek to respond to the movement of the Spirit within the community.

Historical Observance of the Rule of Faith

Such is the Rule of Faith—the one relevant criterion that is to be used to evaluate the validity of any doctrine.

The Rule of Faith must also be applied to the definition of the identity of Christ Jesus. The student of the history of doctrine therefore must ask whether the identity of Christ Jesus in 451 C.E. was simply an authoritative statement by the church, or whether that doctrine was the result of the church's effort to discover the faith that emerged within the community of believers.

However before one attempts to evaluate that doctrine, one might shift the context in an effort to acknowledge the importance that the church has given to that criterion for developing doctrine.

In the late eighth and early ninth centuries Charlemagne changed the political face of Europe. When he began his reign, he held only the northern half of the Frankish kingdom—today's central Germany. Forty-six years later, when he died, his kingdom included most of continental, western Europe. Thus he introduced an expansive worldview to European culture; western Europeans in his time began to think in terms of a great kingdom, no longer only in terms of local folk.

Theology shared in that expansiveness; it began to interpret doctrine with a more expansive worldview. Thus the Rule of Faith was operating: the experience of the believing community, which was modified as a result of Charlemagne's assertiveness, indicated to theologians the need to formulate doctrines that were more expansive than parochial doctrines.[11]

For example Alcuin, the Anglo-Saxon scholar whom Charlemagne asked to interpret the relationship between the emperor and the pope, proposed a new vision of that relationship. Alcuin proposed a new division of authorities. The pope was to lift up his hands to God, as Moses had, for the victory of the empire over the enemies of God and of the church. The emperor on the other hand was to defend the church from the attacks of its pagan foes and to foster the Catholic faith within the church.

In the twelfth century the Christian community found that its belief in the meaning of the eucharistic celebration had shifted: it had come to see the Eucharist as a sacrifice. Consequently, the church used the emerging belief in the Eucharist as sacrifice to recast the doctrine of the Eucharist.[12]

Similarly in the thirteenth century the great scholastic theologian, Thomas Aquinas, acknowledged the significance of the communities' belief as the norm for doctrine. Repeatedly in his *Summa Theologica,* he cites the belief of the community as the standard by which the church was to fashion its doctrine.[13]

Newman: "On Consulting the Faithful in Matters of Doctrine"

In the nineteenth century (1859) John Henry Newman published in the British journal, *The Rambler,* his concept of the Rule of Faith in "On Consulting the Faithful in Matters of Doctrine." He insisted that a development in dogma is discovered only after discussion with the "mind of the Church," that is, with the community of believers. The value that Newman saw in so discovering the mind of the community was that the mind of the community was one of the authoritative witnesses to the tradition of revealed doctrine. Even if there are other witnesses, such as scripture and tradition, Newman judged that the church had given less attention to them and been more respectful of the developing mind of the community. Thus Newman was explicit in insisting that the *consensus* of the community was to be recognized in the expression of doctrine.

Consequently, if the teaching church intends to discover the inspired mind of the church on any question, then the church needs to investigate the mind of the communities of believers. Newman argued that the mind of the faithful was manifest in the communities' public acts—their liturgies, feasts, and prayers. Those acts are testimonies to the teaching of the Holy Spirit: the dogma that the Holy Spirit inspires emerges from the bosom of the church.

To the extent that the church so fashions its doctrine, the church can hope that its teachings can be well received by believers. However to the extent that the church fashions its doctrine from other, noncommunal sources, then it can expect that such teachings will be received by reflective believers with indifference and by those less reflective with superstition.[14]

Though Newman's historically based approach to doctrine was initially—in 1859—rejected by Pope Pius IX, by 1867 the same pope accepted Newman's interpretation of the Rule of Faith as the valid description of the method for formulating doctrine. Pius IX's successor, Leo XIII, raised Newman to the rank of cardinal. Leo thus implied by honoring both Newman and his Rule of Faith that the Roman church was in full agreement with Newman's theology, especially his theology of the formulation of doctrine from the belief of the community of believers.[15]

Vatican Council I (1870) and Consultation of the Faithful

Vatican Council I used Newman's method to hammer out the expression of doctrine. The council met just three years after Pius IX had accepted Newman's criterion for doctrine; it then formulated its own Rule of Faith, which is in harmony with Newman's "On Consulting the Faithful." Vatican Council I had decided, in order to discern doctrine within the community of the faithful, that a doctrine was revealed by God if the consensus of the faithful expressed such belief:

> We believe that revelation is true, not indeed because the intrinsic truth of the mysteries is clearly seen by the natural light of reason, but because of the authority of God who reveals them, for He can neither deceive nor be deceived.
>
> In addition to the internal assistance of His Holy Spirit, it has pleased God to give certain proofs of His revelation, viz. certain Divine facts, especially miracles and prophecies.
>
> Divine revelation is contained in the written books and unwritten traditions.
>
> Vatican Council (1870) I, ii; III, iii[16]

This definition recognized that the church needs to use a method beyond that of reading the Bible or repeating past doctrines in order to identify the self-revelation of God. The more radical method of Vatican I needed to be attentive to "certain proofs of His revelation," which are found not only in "miracles and prophecies," but also in the "unwritten traditions" that are consciously received by the believing community. Vatican I acknowledged that the church is to use the Rule of Faith to discover divine revelation.

Belief as well as doctrine are historical. They include within themselves more than the orthodox tradition of faith. The tradition of orthodox faith is fidelity to the earliest doctrines of the Christian tradition. That faith chooses not to make allowance for the developmental character of Christianity and of belief. However, the Rule of Faith, which recognizes the need to make allowance for historical developments, also recognizes that the history of the believing communities develops and determines changes in doctrines.

Pius XII's Consultation of the Faithful

In November 1940 Pope Pius XII further specified the context in which the Rule of Faith occurs. He taught that the meaning of belief is determined by the teaching of Our Lord, by that of the apostles, by inspired scripture, or by the traditional mores of the holy Fathers and of the church, especially as those are manifested in the liturgy. That was for him the context for *lex orandi, lex credendi* (the Rule of Faith is the rule of doctrine).[17]

Three years later Pius XII again insisted that the liturgy, especially the most ancient Christian liturgies, declares the doctrines of faith.[18]

The first criterion that Pius XII acknowledged as determining doctrine was the worldview that he believed could be traced back to Jesus of Nazareth. Jesus' ministry had been to proclaim, "the Kingdom of God is in your midst," that is, that God is intimately present and active in every experience, thus within the experience of every individual and of every believing community.[19] Because the church in the person of Pius XII agreed that the experiences of life are the self-revelation of God within the world, the church needed to interpret the manner in which God is active and present within the conscious experience of the believing community.

Belief's Determination of Doctrine

Such is precisely the interpretation that is proposed by the Rule of Faith. The teaching function of the church is obliged to address God's self-revelation within the prayer life of the community in order to discover there the orientations that the Spirit may be identifying as dogma. Only when the church's teaching authority has so discovered within the community the self-revelation of God can it formulate dogma that is orthodox.

The Faith of the Community in Relation to Scripture

Pius XII's second criterion for dogma is scripture. However he did not insist that the community was to adapt its belief to scripture. Rather he proposed that the church was to integrate scripture by attending to the prayer life of the community. Apparently he assumed that the community's self-expression in prayer revealed its belief. Consequently communal prayer life had to be consulted before the church was to interpret scripture. The criterion was to be thus not scripture, but rather the belief of the community—the belief of the faithful integrated scripture.

The Gospel of Luke proposes an example of such an approach to using scripture to fashion doctrine: the appearance of the Spirit of the Risen One to the two disciples on the road to Emmaus (Lk 24:13-32) provides the example. In order to appreciate that image of the Spirit's active direction within the community, one needs to be aware of the context into which Luke put the appearance. The two disciples on the journey from Jerusalem to Emmaus did not know that the man who joined them in their journey was the Risen One: "But their eyes were kept from recognizing him" (Lk 24:16). Nonetheless the Risen One, though not recognized, proceeded to influence the conscious faith of the two disciples. "Did not our heart burn within us while he talked to us on the road, while he opened to us the scriptures?" (24:32). Though the identity of the dynamism that had altered their consciousness was not recognized, the Risen One had been actively enlightening them. "And beginning with Moses and all the prophets, he interpreted to them in all the scriptures the things concerning himself" (24:27).

An interpretation of that passage is that Luke is portraying the Risen One as one who no longer walks among the community as he had walked prior to his death. Just as the unrecognized Risen One walked with the two disciples traveling to Emmaus and guided them in their belief, he now walks unrecognized among the community of believers and guides them in their belief. This is Luke's concrete portrayal of the guidance by the Holy Spirit (the Spirit of Christ) from within the experience of the community.

That same guidance is recognized by the Rule of Faith to be the principal criterion of doctrine.

Luke portrays the same guidance in his second book, the Acts of the Apostles. There he portrays the first councils of the disciples as addressing one of the major problems of the early church: whether new Gentile disciples had to become Jews. Luke relates (Acts 15:1–21) that there was within that earliest council sharp disagreement among the leaders of the church. "Some men from Judea," for example, had sought to retain the higher standards of the Law, such as circumcision, for the practice of Christian belief. Nonetheless Luke presents that council as having formulated this decision: "For it has seemed good to the Holy Spirit and to us to lay upon you no greater burden than these necessary things"(Acts 15:28). Evidently those first disciples were confident that the Holy Spirit was so present within their prayerful considerations that they could identify their own consensus as that which "has seemed good to the Holy Spirit." They were able to speak with the assurance that the Holy Spirit was directing them from within their own faith experience.

There is consolation in such a reliance upon the Spirit's activity within the faith life of the community.

However, the Rule of Faith urges that the Spirit can be so discerned only in the plurality of public acts of the community. The apparent security in so focusing is that no private experience of faith apart from the public acts of the community can legitimately claim to be directed by the Spirit. Only the collection of public acts of the believing community can make that claim. Thus the guidance of the Spirit in all of the significant public acts of the community needs to be considered as more significant than the private experiences of faith of an individual. The prestige of the individual is not significant if the church is to discern between those experiences that divinely inspire doctrine and those that an individual directs.[20]

Scripture as the Sole Criterion for Doctrine

The evangelical criterion for faith that Martin Luther (1483–1546) proposed as exhaustive, *"sola scriptura,"* turns to the scriptures alone as the criterion of interpretation. Written scripture alone, but not the self-revealing Word, becomes the norm of faith. That is the difficulty with Luther's revolution of returning to the sources of Christian doctrine: he chose to turn aside from the principal source of doctrine, the Holy Spirit. The Spirit, who acts within the consensus of believers, thus eludes the control of humans. Luther focused on a secondary source, scripture, which is vulnerable to human reasoning and control.

The problem with using only scripture as the one standard for doctrine is that the biblical writers did not, indeed could not, exhaustively articulate the action of the Spirit who guides the community in diverse ways. The norm for belief is not the scriptures, but the Spirit who is actively at work within the believing community. The community therefore needs to strive to discern, in the midst of the community's disagreements and polarities, the traces of the movement of the Spirit.

The guidance of the Spirit, which emerges in the plurality of its witnesses, such as the scriptures, traditional beliefs, or traditional liturgies, acts so that it strives to affect the entire community. That communal effect needs to be considered as primordial in order to discern the content of doctrine that is divinely inspired.

The Prayer Life Continues to Be Cited by Theologians

The Rule of Faith continues to be used to interpret doctrine. There have been major Christian theologians who have cited it since Pius XII's definition of experience as the criterion for doctrine . For example, Edward Schillebeeckx discusses experience in terms of the developmental function of faith,[21] as do James P. Mackey,[22] and Yves Congar.[23]

Process theologians as well have used human experience as their primary point of departure to derive their new doctrine of God. Their point of departure is the modification of every experience by time. For process theologians, time is the parameter of experience that the scientific worldview of the twentieth-century West has introduced and insists on. Thus it is the relative measure for God as for all else. Any human effort to speak about God or the Spirit must relate God and the Spirit to time. Pragmatically the process theologians hold that their reason for insisting upon relativity to time is that time is the necessary context in which to discuss the meaning or the guidance of experience, God, or the Spirit. Everything, including God, must be situated within temporally conditioned human experience.[24]

The Rule of Faith, however, insists that there is always a dialectic, not between the Spirit and time, but the Spirit and human experience. The Spirit guides humans; yet humans remain relatively free to respond or not. In the use of the freedom to respond, the individual can choose to seek to remain on the one hand autonomous to a certain degree and on the other dependent to a certain degree upon the guidance of the Spirit. One might, for example, be aware of one's interior voice summoning one to spend more time with family, but may choose to remain autonomous by deciding to continue to be more distant from family.

Chalcedon's Use of the Rule of Faith

An illustrative example of the application of the Rule of Faith to an ancient Christian doctrine is Chalcedon's doctrine on Jesus Christ as fully human and fully divine. In 451 C.E. the fathers who had assembled at Chalcedon had asserted the paradox that the transcendental one is united with Jesus, a historical person. Jesus was a human individual, dependent and relative, as are all humans; yet Jesus was, for the Council of Chalcedon, also the absolute God.

The question that the fathers of the Council of Chalcedon had to answer was how they might articulate the paradox of belief in Christ. By using the Rule of Faith, they hoped to discover how the believing community might lead them to express the community's dialectical doctrine about Jesus Christ.

A doctrine about the identity of Jesus, as any doctrine, is supposed to be a consequence of the application of the Rule of Faith. If the articulation of a doctrine about Jesus by Chalcedon was to be accepted by the believing community, then the fathers at Chalcedon were required to situate that doctrine within the context and the experience of the conscious belief of the community—doctrine had to be situated both within the historical circumstances in which Christians found themselves and within their response to the preaching about Jesus. The conscious, Christian faith of the fifth-century community of believers had been constituted both by the self-revealing Word active within the community and by the historical events that had formed the community. The Rule of Faith challenged the fathers to discover and to respect that relationship if they were to express the Spirit's doctrine about the Word.

Thus the fathers of the Council were obliged first to interweave their sensitivity to the New Testament's first-century portrayal of Jesus' proclamation with their respect for the fifth-century experience of the believing community. Next the fathers needed to interrelate fifth-century scholarly reflection on scripture with fifth-century communal experience of belief. Finally they needed to interrelate the believing community's moral customs with the wider cultural experiences of fifth-century culture.

That would have to be the approach that the fathers needed to take in order to interpret God's self-revelation according to the Rule of Faith if they hoped to assert a doctrine that was acceptable to believers in that historical period. Believers would be able to grasp the Council's doctrine if the Council used current symbols that the Spirit had been presenting to them within their experience of Christian belief. The Rule has always directed that such an effort be made to integrate the cultural context, the belief of the community of the faithful, and the traditions of belief.

The Rule of Faith in the Twentieth Century

Hence the Rule even now requires the American church in the late twentieth century to formulate its dogma so that its doctrine reflects the American context of a twentieth-century, western, pragmatic experience of belief. That pragmatism affects the American believing community's manner of understanding the symbols of belief differently from the manner that the endemic attitudes of other communities lead those communities to understand the same symbols of belief. Thus, the integration of cultural context, belief, and the traditional symbols of belief results in an integration of a doctrine. Doctrine needs to articulate a fundamental attitude toward life that is specific for an individual community. The community has inherited from its culture the context that situates any doctrine that it might embrace.

The church had attempted to identify its doctrines as determined by the Spirit active within the belief of the community. As a result, the church could hope authoritatively to teach doctrines as determined not by ecclesiastical powers, but by those who gather to worship. The community can then be expected to assimilate as expressions of its belief those doctrines that portray what it had been experientially believing. However the community is not likely to assimilate as expressions of its belief those doctrines portraying that which neither it nor other contemporary communities experientially believe. The Word is relatively active in the community; it directs each community to assimilate or to ignore a doctrine insofar as that doctrine reflects the belief that the Spirit has inspired within a specific community.

Pastoral Need to Consult the Faithful

In a case in which a doctrine is ignored by the community, then the teaching authority of the church needs to reexamine the doctrine in terms of whether or not it is in harmony with the Spirit who is active within the belief of the community.

In a case in which a firm conviction regarding a doctrine has continued within the community, then the church can conclude that the doctrine was formulated in harmony with the Spirit's revelation of the contours of that doctrine within the belief of the community.

Nonetheless the converse might be the case: the community may not be convinced that a doctrine is valid. The 1870 doctrine of infallibility comes to mind: the communities of believers, especially after *Humanae Vitae,* the 1968 encyclical on contraception, are much less ready to confess the infallibility of papal doctrine than had been the case in the late nineteenth century. The church can conclude that the doctrine is no longer in harmony with the Spirit's guidance of the belief of the community.

By attending to the community's consciousness of its embrace of doctrines, the teaching authority can discern which doctrines have received their formulations from the Spirit. It can also discern which doctrines need to be reinterpreted.

Theological Need to Assess Current Doctrines by the Rule of Faith

The Rule of Faith requires that all doctrines, not only the doctrine of Chalcedon, be open to possible reformulation. Doctrine can be considered as securely determined by the Spirit, continuing to inspire belief in that doctrine within the consciousness of the believing community. Yet the Rule demands of the church a sensitivity to the Spirit's working in the community's consciousness. Such a sensitivity may reveal that the Spirit is moving the teaching church to reformulate a doctrine.

Because the Spirit is so active, the Rule challenges the church to acknowledge that the highest authority for doctrine is neither scripture nor tradition, but the activity of the Spirit within the community.

Such an interpretation of the Rule of Faith opens up the possibility that previously formulated doctrine, the interpretation of scripture, the gender of the priest, or the teaching authority of the church are not closed to criticism according to the Spirit's inspiration of the community.

If the church is to give itself to the task of discovering the inspiration of the Spirit within the community of believers, it needs to turn to the public acts of the community. The interrelationship of those public acts with the inspiration that the Holy Spirit has given to the community of believers must be used as the principle norm for the formulation of doctrine.

Consequently one who critically reflects upon the validity of a particular doctrine, for example, the virginity of Mary, Mary as the mother of God, or Chalcedon's definition of the identity of Jesus, needs to discern how the community expressed its belief at the time that those doctrines were formulated.

A Theology of Hermeneutics

The Rule of Faith is thus a hermeneutical principle of interpretation. That hermeneutic is the effort to discern whether interpretations of doctrine were offered by the Spirit, actively inspiring belief within a particular time by means of the assembly of experiences that form the conscious belief of that Christian community. That hermeneutic intends to discern the source of doctrines within the community's belief, to discern the authority that the community might recognize a doctrine to have, and to discern whether a community uses its assumed worldview to fashion its scientific paradigms and its religious doctrines. Moreover the community's experiences of belief, of authority, and of the relevance of reason or of science to doctrine can be judged to witness to the Spirit's inspiration of faith within the community. Those experiences witness to the Spirit's inspiration to the extent that one has discerned how each is considered in relation to the others.[25]

Thus the authority for interpretation is not located only in primitive writings (the sacred scriptures), nor in past events (the life of Jesus), nor in authoritative formulas (official, ecclesiastical, dogmatic definitions), nor in a particular functional authority (the pope). Authority for interpretation is located in none of these alone, but in all of these together insofar as they are validated within the community's conscious, cultural experience of belief. Within that context those criteria form the contours from which belief the church can formulate valid doctrine for the believing community.

Insofar as the teaching authority of the church has recognized that its doctrines must be fashioned from such a context, then to that extent it can speak of its doctrine as revealed by the Spirit who is active within the world (the Rule of Faith). Then the church's doctrinal tradition can cite its doctrine as teaching that has been received from God.

III. Early Hymns—A Preface to a Dialectical Interpretation of the Meaning of Christ Jesus

Did the Council of Chalcedon's definition of Christ Jesus faithfully reflect the belief of the community or did the Council's bishops impose their doctrinal formulation? If the bishops at the Council were careful to reflect the belief of the community, the community could have recognized the expression of their belief in the doctrine. Then the community would have been able to confess that doctrine as the expression of a belief inspired by the Holy Spirit. If, however, the bishops imposed a doctrine that was different from the belief of the community, then the believers would have had serious difficulty in confessing that doctrine.

Therefore one needs to find some access to the data about the pre-Chalcedonian community's belief in Christ Jesus.

Let us assume that the early Christian hymns about Christ Jesus reveal the active belief of the communities that were using those hymns. Thus, the belief manifested in those early hymns can be used as a criterion to judge whether the doctrine of the bishops at Chalcedon succeeded in presenting the community with a doctrine that reflected the community's belief. Perhaps we will discover that the Council attempted (1) to repeat the early church's belief; (2) to express the fifth-century church's belief; or (3) to find a convergence between the early church's belief and the fifth-century church's belief.

Before reflecting upon those hymns, the reader might well be forewarned: the hymns reveal a sophisticated early belief in Christ.

The earliest Christian hymns are startling: at first reading they seem to support the heretical conclusion of Arius and of his follower Diosthenes, both of whom apparently reflected faithfully the way in which the earliest Christians identified Christ Jesus. The early hymns praised Christ as Savior, Redeemer, the Son of God, and the pinnacle of humanity. Thus there appears initially to be no reason to criticize Arius; his identification of Christ seems to have mirrored that of the earliest Christian community.

However upon closer examination everything changes. The study of the hymns discloses a critical distinction. Whereas the early Christian hymns indeed offer praise to a Christ who is Savior, Redeemer, and the pinnacle of humanity, they also suggest, even if they do not explicitly express it, that Christ is to be imagined as much more than a human being. One could not conclude from the earliest Christian hymns that Christ could not be divine, yet the Arians reached that conclusion. They insisted that "there was when he was not." He was not eternal, but temporal. He had been begotten by the Father before the ages. Therefore he could not possibly be identical with the eternal divinity.

Early Belief as a Dialectic

The critical difference between the earliest Christian hymns' identification of Christ Jesus and that of the Arians is *method*. Those who praised Christ with the earliest hymns confessed Christ by means of a dialectical tension between reason and imagination. The Arians on the other hand insisted on confessing Christ in the univocal category constructed by syllogistic reasoning. They situated the identification of Christ within the clarity of logic: what was said of Christ needed to be expressed in a logical manner that eliminated any need to appeal to mystery. This difference between the dialectical method of the earliest hymns and the logical clarity of the Arians is critical.

The earliest Christian hymns confessed an imaginative, Christian faith in Jesus as Lord. Dialectical faith is a confession of belief in both sides of a paradox—the human Jesus is also the divine Jesus—without resolving the tension within that paradox. Since faith is assent to that which cannot be proven, the communities who used those hymns assented to the meaning of Christ that they could imagine, but not demonstrate. The Arians on the other hand expressed their faith as their logically reasoned identification of Christ. They would assent only to the Christ whom they could identify by logical inference.

This difference is no less critical for Christians in the late twentieth century. Many people insist that they can infer the identity of Christ Jesus from carefully reasoned logical inferences; those people are very much like the Arians. Other people identify Christ in a confession of faith. They do not put aside their human categories of logic and rational categories. Nevertheless they understand that the Christian manner of identifying Christ is not only through rational categories, but also through imaginative belief. Belief expressed imaginatively successfully confesses the Christ who eludes the categories of rational argument.

Contemporary Faith as a Dialectic

The thesis of this book is that twentieth-century Christians, no less than the early Christians who used the hymns, must identify Christ dialectically. To the extent we confess Christ with the crisp clarity of rational argument, we are not uniting with the earliest Christian believers, but are close to the followers of Arius. We become rationalists, not fideists. Such people simply refuse to enter into the ambiguous domain of religious faith in their confession of the meaning of Christ Jesus. Christians today, no less than in the era after the Council of Chalcedon (451 C.E.), are able to remain faithful to the Christian tradition while identifying themselves as members of the surrounding culture. However they can do so only if they confess Christ not only with logical argument, but also with an imaginative religious faith. They need logic and analysis to understand empirical data, but also need imagination to assent to the Christ who eludes the categories of human knowledge.

However there are Christians who insist that they confess Christ only from the perspective of faith. While they retain their rightful claim to be members of the believing community, they abdicate the use of reason and thus their claim to be members of a community that is committed to the culture of the late twentieth century. In fact they have abdicated any claim to be associated with the members of the community of believers in the second half of the fifth century: the Council of Chalcedon challenged the church to be faithful not only to those assertions accessible by imaginative religious belief, but also to assertions accessible by rational categories. Intelligent Christian believers use the tension of that dialectic in the confession of Christ Jesus.

Summing Up

We can draw a brief profile of the changes that we will look at more closely in the coming chapters.

1. The sophisticated expression of belief in the early hymns is developed further in the shift in the theology of the

hymns after the Council of Nicaea (325 C.E.). The Council condemned the Arian doctrine concerning Christ Jesus and insisted that God and Christ Jesus share the same substance. As a result the post-Nicaean hymns took on a polemical tone that they had not had previously. They appear to be less expressions of spontaneous faith, as they had been, and more an expression similar to the theology of orthodox doctrine formulated by the Council of Nicaea.

That orthodoxy, expressed in hymns, repeated the Nicene assertion that God and Christ Jesus shared the same substance. One suspects that the anti-Arian bishops had taken over the task of composing hymns that Christian communities were to use in their worship.

2. A hundred years later, after the Council of Chalcedon, the tone of Christian hymns again shifted. The hymns used after 451 C.E. articulated less poetry, but more polemical theology that mirrored the theology which the Council of Chalcedon had developed. In becoming polemically theological, the hymns moved further away from the spontaneous expression of communal belief, their tone in the first two centuries of the Christian tradition.

However that is a digression from the thesis. The issue this book argues is that the Christian manner of identifying Christ has been and is a dialectic between reason and the imagination of faith.

IV. The Pre-Nicaean Hymns Concerning Christ and the Belief Expressed in Those Early Hymns

Dialectical Belief of the Earliest Christian Hymns

The thesis that the earliest Christian hymns witness to the dialectical faith of the earliest believers needs to be defended by reflecting on the hymns themselves and by identifying the faith that they articulated.

The purpose of this study is to interpret those early hymns by the Rule of Faith: those early hymns reveal the faith that the Spirit was fashioning in the earliest community of believers in Christ Jesus.

The Arian Hymn, *Thalia* (319-45 C.E.)

The context for the study of the early Christian hymns is the controversy that became focused as the Arian controversy: namely, the disagreement concerning the identity of Jesus Christ. In the fourth century Arius insisted that Christ could be Redeemer, Prophet, and even Son of God; however he could not be God. Nevertheless the hymns from the centuries prior to Arius portray Jesus Christ in much more ambiguous tones.

The following hymn is most important in that it is the one extant expression by Arius of his own doctrine. Arius acknowledged that, though Christ may indeed be the origin of creation, the one who was "adopted" to be God's Son, nevertheless he cannot be one who could be equal to God. Nor could he be one who has the same substance as God. Rather, God before creation made the Son to be the origin of creation.

Arius's hymn is full-blown theological polemic.

Thalia (The Banquet)

According to the faith of God's elect,
Who know God, holy children,
Sound in their creed,
Gifted with the Holy Spirit of God,

I have received these things from the partakers of wisdom,
Accomplished, taught of God, and altogether wise.
Along their track I have pursued my course with like opinions,
I, the famous among men, the much-suffering for God's glory;
And, taught of God, I have gained wisdom and knowledge,

That God made the Son the origin of creation,
Being Himself unoriginate, and adopted Him to be His Son;
Who on the other hand, has no property of divinity
In His own Hypostasis,
Not being equal, nor consubstantial with Him;

That God is invisible, not only to the creatures
Created through the Son, but to the Son Himself;

That there is a Trinity, but not with an equal glory,
The Hypostases being incommunicable with each other,
One infinitely more glorious than the other;

That the Father is foreign in substance to the Son,
As existing unoriginate;
That by God's will the Son became Wisdom, Power,
The Spirit, the Truth, the Word, the Glory, and the Image of God;
That the Father, as being Almighty, is able to give existence
To a being equal to the Son, though not superior to Him;
That, from the time that He was made, being a mighty God,
He has hymned the praises of His Superior;

That He cannot investigate His Father's nature,
It being plain that the originated cannot comprehend the
        unoriginate;
Nay, that He does not know His own.[1]

Arius prayed emphatically that, because God made the Son to be the origin of creation, therefore Christ "has no property of divinity" in himself. For Arius the Son could not know God with the interior knowledge that God has of the divine self. The hymn explicitly asserts that God is superior to Christ; this was for Arius one of many signs that Christ is the inferior of God and could not therefore be God.

Arius does identify Christ as the origin of creation and as the adopted Son of God. However he was careful to deny that Christ deserves to be identified as someone other than an intermediary between God and humans. Arius refused to consider that Christ could be identified with God.

In contrast to the earlier hymnmakers, Arius did not tolerate a tensive faith that both rationally confessed Christ and imaginatively trusted in him with belief. For Arius either Christ was *not* divine, or he *was* divine. He had no tolerance for an unresolved tension in the confession of Christ as both human and divine. Arius therefore insisted on reducing Christ to the status of one who was more than human, yet not one who was equal with God. Therefore for Arius, Christ was nondivine.

Earliest Hymns' Portrayal of Jesus

The earliest Christian hymns confess a faith in the identity of Jesus as the Proclaimer who redeemed, saved, revealed, and uplifted. Jesus was the source and cause of human hope. He assured humanity that all sins have been forgiven.

Such an identification of Christ Jesus in the hymns allows the conclusion that the early Christians believed Christ Jesus to be one who had accomplished more for the human family than a human individual was able to accomplish; namely, he had somehow been able to save every human individual from sin. Thus the issue for this study is that the earliest believers restricted the identity of Christ Jesus—a restriction of Jesus as no more than a unique human. They had not formulated such a restriction. On the contrary they acknowledged that because of what he accomplished, he had a unique relationship with God.

The Development of Hymns from Confessions of Belief to Theological Arguments

The early hymns appear to be confessions of belief in terms of images drawn from Old Testament sources or from cultural images. They reveal the faith of the people who used them to color their worship services with poetic expressions of their assertion of belief in Christ Jesus and in the God of Christ Jesus.

However the color of the hymns gradually changed from such a confession of belief to a more polemical theology, reflecting accepted doctrine regarding the identity of Christ Jesus. These later, more theological hymns show less a color of communal worship in trust, but more a color of polemical debate with doctrines that are not accepted by the persons who had fashioned the hymns.

**Earliest Hymns: Pre-New Testament Hymn:
"The Great Hallel"**

"The Great Hallel" passed from its use in Jewish worship services to use in the earliest worship services of the church. The community of believers had chosen to imitate the song supposedly used by Christ Jesus and his disciples in the hymn that they had sung when they left the upper room, after they had observed the Passover, and as they went out to the Mount of Olives (Mt 26:30). The ritual of the celebration of the Passover included "the Great Hallel"

> consisting of Psalms 113 to 118 inclusive. The 113th and 114th were sung previous to the feast; the others, after it. We thus know, with singular accuracy, what was the first hymn of praise in the Christian Church.[2]

Though one might judge that the author, Samuel Willoughby Duffield, is rather sentimental in that assessment, still one can appreciate the historical positioning of "the Great Hallel," that is, the Hallelujah, in the worship services of the early Christian church.

Duffield went on to identify "the earliest received anthems....There were, indeed, in the primitive church, eight of these classic expressions of worship:

1. The Lesser Doxology (*Gloria Patri*),
2. The Greater Doxology (*Gloria in Excelsis*),
3. The *Ter Sanctus,*
4. The Hallelujah (Psalm 113),
5. The *Nunc Dimittis,*
6. The *Benedicite,*
7. The *Magnificat,*
8. The *Te Deum.*"[3]

However one might assess the status of "received" anthems, one might nonetheless appreciate the status of those hymns, which include the Hallelujah of Psalm 113, as among the earliest hymns of praise of the church.

"Hallelujah" was apparently used as a hymn to Jesus Risen by his first followers. After his crucifixion they had no doubt experienced desperation because of the loss of their unique leader. Then to their great surprise and amazement they experienced within their midst the presence of the Risen One. Thus they introduced into their worship the great Hallel, that is, Psalm 113, "Hallelujah," which is the opening line of Psalm 113: "Praise the Lord." That triumphant Jewish exclamation articulated the characteristic of the earliest disciples' belief—that their Lord continued to be present with them even after his death.

The Hallelujah has never been dropped from the liturgy. It continues to express not only the eschatological triumph of Jesus Risen, but also the hope with which Jesus transformed the lives of those who initially were transfixed by the desperation of the crucifixion.[4]

The proclamation "Hallelujah"—Psalm 113:

> *The Great Hallel (Hallelujah!)—Psalm 113*
> [1] Hallelujah! [trans.: Praise the Lord!]
> Praise, O servants of the Lord,
> Praise the name of the Lord!
> [2] Blessed be the name of the Lord
> from this time forth and for evermore!
> [3] From the rising of the sun to its setting
> the name of the Lord is to be praised!
> [4] The Lord is high above all nations,
> and his glory above the heavens!
> [5] Who is like the Lord our God,
> who is seated on high,
> [6] who looks far down upon the heavens and the earth?
> [7] He raises the poor from the dust,
> and lifts the needy from the ash heap,

⁸ to make them sit with princes,
with the princes of his people.
⁹ He gives the barren woman a home,
making her the joyous mother of children.
Hallelujah!

(trans. RSV, 1973)

Some of those verses deserve comment, since the earliest Christian communities had used them to "Praise the Lord," Jesus Christ:

> the Lord is praised forevermore (113:2);
> the Lord is high above the nations (113:4);
> the Lord is like the Lord our God (113:5);
> the Lord raises the poor from the dust (113:7).

Evidently the earliest Christians, in applying Psalm 113 to Jesus, were recognizing him as far more than a human Savior, but even as one "high above the nations" and "like the Lord our God" who transformed their lives from the shadow of desperation to the light of hope.

Earliest Hymns: The New Testament Hymns

Philippians 2:6–11

May you have in you the same mind as Christ Jesus had,
Who though he was in the form of God
Did not count equality with God a thing to be grasped,
But emptied himself,
Taking the form of a servant,
Being born in the likeness of men.
And being found in human form,
He humbled himself and became obedient unto death,
Even death on a cross.
Therefore God has highly exalted him
And bestowed on him the name which is above every name,
So that at the name of Jesus Christ

Every knee should bow
In heaven, on earth and under the earth
And every tongue confess that Jesus Christ is Lord,
To the glory of God the Father.

(trans. DPL)

This hymn is thought by some historians to have appeared in the very earliest eucharistic celebrations of the communities of Christians. Regardless of whether or not this hymn was used prior to its appearance in Paul's letter, it does appear to have been used thereafter in some of the early liturgies of worship of Christ Jesus.

The hymn praises Christ as one who preexisted as God (v. 6). It praises him as having existed in the actual likeness of man (v. 7). It recognizes a unique relationship between God and Christ in that God has highly exalted him and bestowed on him that name which is above every name: "Jesus Christ is Lord" (v. 11).

1 Peter 2:22–25

The First Letter of Peter, a very early Christian document, can be dated at about 90 C.E. Within the letter is an early hymn concerning Christ Jesus:

> [22] He committed no sin; no guile was found on his lips. [23] When he was reviled, he did not revile in turn; when he suffered, he did not threaten. But he trusted to him who judges justly. [24] He himself bore our sins in his body on the tree, that we might die to sin and live to righteousness. [25] "By his wounds you have been healed." For you were straying like sheep, but now have been returned to the shepherd and guardian of your souls.

The hymn's initial reflection on Christ is that Christ Jesus was human. Yet he was innocent; in him there was no guile.

However, the conventional judgment regarding the human being who suffers is that one had sinned and has manifested consequently varieties of guile (v. 22). Then the hymn reflects further upon Jesus' moral, human stature in that he treated all well, rather than with the vengeance that those who treated him shamefully deserved (v. 23).

At that point the hymn shifts its focus to praise Christ Jesus as being more than human. For because he bore our sins in his body, we, though previously guilty, now live with hope. Because he was able to bear the sins of humanity, Christ Jesus is the Redeemer of all. Therefore he was unique.

It would be incomprehensible to claim that a mere human could have so transformed the destiny of all humanity. The hymn suggests a dialectical belief: that Christ Jesus is somehow divine as well as human.

1 Timothy 3:16

The hymn in 1 Timothy 3 identifies Christ Jesus as a man with extraordinary qualities:

> He was manifested in the flesh,
> vindicated in the Spirit,
> seen by the angels,
> preached among the nations, (3:16a)

Then however the hymn moves beyond the category of Christ as human, to Christ as

> Believed on in the world and
> Taken up in glory. (3:16b)

These last two confessions suggest that he is extraordinary—his destiny after death was to be taken into glory, that is, he received a glory that no human could hope to attain alone.

Earliest Hymns: The Letter to the Colossians' Early Christian Hymn:

Colossians 1:15-20

[15] He is the image of the invisible God, the firstborn of all creation, [16] indeed in him all things were created, in heaven and on the earth—things visible and invisible; whether thrones or dominions, principalities or powers— all things were created through him and for him. [17] He is before all things, and in him all things hold together. [18] He is the head of the body the church; he is the beginning, the firstborn from the dead—that in everything he might be preeminent. [19] For in him all the fullness of God was pleased to dwell, [20] and through him to reconcile to himself all things, whether on earth, or in heaven—making peace by the blood of his cross.

The initial identification of Christ Jesus here is that he is "the image of the invisible God" (v. 15), that is, the one who images God for humans. That need not be interpreted to signify that Christ is God.

In fact, the second identification— "the firstborn of all creation" (v. 15)—identifies Christ in terms of the Hebrew "firsts," such as the first fruits of agriculture. The "firsts" were consecrated to God as a sign that God is master of the earth. So Christ is "the firstborn of all creation," in other words, consecrated to God as a sign that God is the master of humankind. Thus Christ as "the firstborn of all creation" represents the human community to God.

The hymn goes on to identify Christ Jesus as the word and wisdom that God used to create all things (v. 16), as he who is before all things (v. 17), as he who is the head of the church, the beginning, the firstborn from the dead, the preeminent one, and the one in whom the fullness of God is pleased to dwell (vv. 18-19). Nonetheless the hymn leaves ambiguous the judgment that he is God, that his substance is the divine substance, or that his self is the divine self. The poem is content to affirm that Christ is human and in some incomprehensible way is at the same time the supreme one, the one who is above the human level. There the confession of Colossians ceases: the faith remains hidden by a veil of dialectic—the Christ is identified as not only human, but as also, in some way one can only imagine, the image of the divine.

The precise identification of Christ is not there reduced to a human category. The hymn confesses a belief that moves between the dual identities of Christ without attempting to reduce the identity of Christ to the level of human understanding.

Earliest Hymns: The Early Hymn in the Gospel of John

In the Gospel of John—written in the early second century—there is a text that appears to have been an early Christological hymn, John's Prologue. It has the character of a hymn in its deliberate attention to the images of light, darkness, and life. Just as hymns build their verses around such images, so does this passage tend to focus the attention of its readers. The evangelist reworked the hymns for his Prologue in order to personify Christ in the wisdom tradition.

The Gospel of John—Prologue (Jn 1:1-14)
[1]In the beginning was the word; the word was with God; and the word was God. [2]He was in the beginning with God. [3]All things were made through him; and without him there was nothing that was made. [4]In him was life; and the life was the light of humankind. [5]The light shines in the darkness; and the darkness has not overcome it. [6]There was a man sent from God whose name was John. [7]This man came, that he might bear witness to the light, so that all might believe through him. [8]He was not the light, but came to bear witness to the light. [9]The true light that illumines everyone was coming into the world. [10]He

was in the world; the world was made through him. Yet the world ignored him. [11]He came onto his own people; yet his own did not receive him. [12]But to all who do receive him, who believe in his name, he gives power to become children of God. [13]These were born not of blood, nor of the will of the flesh, nor of the will of man, but of God. [14]And the word was made flesh, and dwelt amongst us, full of grace and truth; we have beheld his glory, glory as of the only Son from the Father.

John used this hymn as his prologue to identify Christ Jesus as one who is far more than human—as the one who had been with God at the time of creation. He was the Word by whom God made all that was made (vv. 1-3).

Moreover the hymn identifies Christ as the light that even in the present illumines everyone. Thus Christ is identified as clearly beyond any category that humans can affirm about one another (vv. 4-5).

Furthermore he is identified as the Word made flesh, as the only Son from the Father, even as the one through whom all grace and truth come to humanity (vv. 14-17).

In applying such images to Christ Jesus, the hymn confesses Christ Jesus as possessing a unique, divine power. That power is the consequence of his being made not only according to human flesh, but also of his being somehow identified as the unique Word who was with God.

Earliest Hymns: The Early Second Century Letter to the Hebrews—Another Hymn to Christ:

Hebrews 1:3
He reflects the glory of God and bears the very stamp of his nature, upholding the universe by his word of power. When he had made purification for sins, he sat down at the right hand of the Majesty on high. (Heb 1:3)

This remnant of an earlier hymn praises Christ who, though he has a unique relationship with God our Father, has an identity that remains tensive.

The word "tensive" is used to identify a confession of belief in Christ that maintains the tension between confessing Christ as the one whom rational knowledge can acknowledge him to be, a human individual, and the one whom imaginative belief acknowledges him to be. He is the Christ whom God had sent as God's own representative or God's Christ, who worked human salvation and who remains present in the human community. That is, he both reflects God's glory and accomplished purification for sins (suffered crucifixion).

Because the hymn from the Letter to the Hebrews leaves his identity unspecified, therefore, the belief of the hymn also remains tensive. It praises him both as somehow united with God and as united with those who suffer death.

One would be presumptuous to use this fragment to say more than that there is a relationship between the God and Jesus—a relationship between the One chosen to be the image of God and the One who is God's self. Just as the hymn does not presume to reduce that relationship to logical categories, so one cannot use the ambiguity of this hymn fragment to analyze a rational conclusion about that relationship.

Other Very Early Hymns

The *Phos Hilaron* is cited by Basil of Caesarea in the fourth century as a hymn that was then widely known and that previously had been known in the ancient church. Apparently it was used in the Christian rituals within the catacombs of the second century as part of the liturgy during the lighting of candles at sunset.[5]

Phos Hilaron (O Radiant Light!!)

O radiant Light, O Son divine of God the Father's
deathless face,

O image of the Light sublime that fills the heavenly
dwelling place.

O Son of God, the source of life, Praise is your due by
night and day.

Our happy lips must raise the strain of your esteemed
and splendid name.

Lord Jesus Christ, as daylight fades, as shine the lights of
eventide,

We praise the Father with the Son, the Spirit blest, and
with them one.

(trans. DPL)

This most ancient Christian hymn identifies Christ Jesus
as "radiant light" who is the "Son divine" of the Father. Moreover the author believed that light to be so sublime that it "fills
the heavenly dwelling place." The Christian communities that
used this hymn had come to believe that the relationship
between Christ Jesus and God was less than dialectical and
ambiguous, but somehow more of a relationship between two
divine Ones.

Another very early hymn, *Bridle of Steeds Untamed,* was
attached to the *Paedagogos* ("The Doctrine on Christian Living"), attributed to Clement of Alexandria (c. 150–215). Its
vocabulary and phraseology are well adapted to the Gnosti-
cism of the second century. However it also articulated a
dialectical and trusting belief in Christ Jesus, both human, as
the Shepherd, the Fisher of Souls, and divine, as the Everlasting Word.

Bridle of Steeds Untamed
Bridle of steeds untamed
Wing of flightless nestlings,

> Sure rudder of untried youth,
> Shepherd of royal sheep[6]
> (trans. DPL)

This hymn preserves the tradition of a dialectical Christian belief. Its theme is to praise Christ Jesus by identifying him again as the most extraordinary of humans. Indeed so extraordinary is Christ the Redeemer, that he is the "Shepherd of royal sheep"—somehow he has been able to communicate to his followers a participation in his own royal bloodline. Yet there was no effort made by the hymnmaker to claim that the human mind is capable of identifying precisely the relationship between Christ and God.

Later Hymns: The *Odes of Solomon*

A scroll of hymns, composed in approximately 65 C.E. by a Jewish convert to Christianity, but unknown until its discovery in 1909, contained forty-one odes for use as hymns in Palestinian-Christian congregations. The composer used the pseudonym "Solomon" perhaps as a sign that the hymns' images were taken from the Old Testament, most especially from the love poetry of the Song of Solomon.

The writing of these hymns by the mythical Solomon, who shared the identity of one who lived in the tenth century before Christ with that of the author in the first century after Christ, contributes a special mystical character to the hymns.[7]

The poet confessed in these odes that Christ Jesus is the unique Savior. Christ is the crown who is identified with each human (*Ode* 1)[8] He is both the one who is loved and the model of human love (*Ode* 3). Thus, he manifested himself as human. Consequently, the odes urge humans to trust that, just as Christ their brother is in a unique relationship with God, so too they have been placed in the same relationship (*Ode* 7). The odes thus insist that Christ has accomplished for all humans a status that only God (or one through whom God uniquely worked) would have been capable of achieving for them.

He is savior ("I captured the world...for the glory of the Most High") and the Son of God ("God my Father"). (*Ode* 10). These confessions of Christ as Savior and as Son of God, imaginative assertions by the mystical Solomon about the unique relationship between Christ and the God, are not philosophical assertions from which logical conclusions can be analyzed. Rather they are assertions that reveal a belief in the Christ who as both Son of God and Savior is identified as the one sent by God to be God's chosen one among humans, to be one who stands in a unique position within the human community. He had become for the communities who used those hymns the individual who was also the unique agent of God.

Then in *Ode* 17 Solomon writes "And he glorified me by his kindness, and raised my understanding to the height of truth." In that confession of faith Solomon asserts Christ's glorious status and his understanding that was elevated above the human level.

Nonetheless there were individuals who insisted on reducing such statements by Solomon to an analysis which concluded that God had "elevated" Christ to the status of God. Those were the "adoptionists." They analyzed the hymn so as to conclude that Christ was not God in virtue of his own inherent self, but had become God after his life of faithful response.

Yet, *Ode* 17 repeats the images used by Paul the apostle and John the evangelist; namely, the images of Christ as the head of the mystical body (Rom 12) and as the vine (Jn 15). Both of these place Christ as supreme above human identity, as elevated above all humans and even as capable of uniting all humans with himself and thus with the God with whom he is uniquely related.

Briefly *Ode* 19 refers to God as the *One* who participated in the virgin birth of Christ from Mary: Christ is unique among

humans. Next, *Ode* 22 proclaims Christ as having preexisted his
birth. *Ode* 24 then praises Christ, who at his baptism was in
union with "the dove," presumably, the Holy Spirit. *Ode* 28:
Christ lived out the promises of second Isaiah's Suffering Servant. *Ode* 31: Christ spoke in the place of God—he acted as one
who revealed God's innermost thoughts. *Ode* 36: Christ was the
supreme human person. *Ode* 41: Christ preexisted his birth in
union with God; he is Savior, Man, Son of the Most High, Messiah. *Ode* 42: Christ is the way to God, the risen one, the one
who lovingly forgave his persecutors, and the Son of God.

Ode 1

The Lord is on my head like a crown
And I shall never be without him.
But thou livest upon my head
And have blossomed upon me.
Thy fruits are full and complete;
They are full of my salvation.

Ode 3

I am putting on the love of the Lord,
For I should not have known how to love the Lord,
If he had not continuously loved me.
I love the Beloved and I myself love him,
And where his nest is, there also am I.
And I shall be no stranger,
Because there is no jealousy
With the Lord Most High and Merciful.
I have been united to him
Because the lover has found the beloved.
Because I love him that is the Son,
I shall become a son.

Ode 7

Open, open your hearts to the exultation of the Lord,
And let your love abound from the heart to the lips.

You who were despised, from henceforth be lifted up.
For your righteousness has been lifted up;
For the right hand of the Lord is with you,
And he will be your Helper.

. . . .

[Christ speaks]

. . . .

For I turn not my face from my own,
Because I know them
And before they had existed,
I recognized them;
And imprinted a seal on their faces.
I fashioned their members,
And my own breasts I prepared for them,
That they might drink my holy milk and live by it.
I am pleased by them,
And am not ashamed by them.
For my workmanship are they,
And the strength of my thoughts.

Ode 10

I took courage and became strong
And captured the world,
And it became mine for the glory of the Most High
And of God my Father.

Ode 17

And He who knew and exalted men,
Is the Most High in all his perfection.
And he glorified me by his kindness,
And raised my understanding to the height of truth.
And I went toward all my bondsmen in order to loose them;
That I might not leave anyone bound or binding.
Because they became my members,
And I was their head.

(trans. DPL)

The Arian Issue—Reducing the Meaning of Christ to Human Categories

The critical figure of Arius (c. 250-336) looms as the background for fourth-century theology: the theology of that century is comprehensible only in relation to him. In order to comprehend the early church's belief in Christ Jesus, one needs to be aware of Arius's impact upon the belief of the early church.

Arius was probably from Libya, near Egypt. After studying theology in Antioch, he returned to Egypt as a charismatic priest, widely and effectively promulgating his doctrine: Jesus Christ may indeed have been the Redeemer, even the Savior, but could not have been God. By 323 his doctrine had spread throughout the eastern and southern coast of the Mediterranean. Thereafter church belief in Jesus Christ took on the form of a struggle between the followers of Arius, the Arians, and the believers who confessed Jesus Christ as God. From the early fourth century until the sixth century, that struggle greatly influenced the belief in Christ that was expressed in the hymns of the church.

Arius and his followers had redefined the issue. They restricted the meaning of Christ to what they could infer concerning Christ and God using logical analysis. They chose to assume, as the early Christian hymns had not, that the significance of Jesus Christ could and should be situated within human, analytical categories. Even the Arian confession of Christ as Savior and Redeemer insisted that Jesus could not have been God. They assumed that the identity of Christ Jesus must be restricted to a definite category within the envelope of human experience and comprehension. Arius and his followers refused to acknowledge the validity of the challenge of the authoritative confessions about Jesus in early Christian hymns; namely, their identity of Christ as divine. The Arians chose rather to trust in the sufficiency of their own logic that the identity of Christ Jesus could not be more than that of a divine human. Perhaps indeed he was a unique Son of God, even a Savior, but nonetheless not God.

The Arians did not confess their belief in Christ with a dialectical ambiguity about Christ's identity; they were not modest enough to employ the ambiguity that the early Christian hymns used in their confession of belief in Christ. Rather they moved the identification of Christ into the domain of reason and insisted upon limiting him to a category that human reason was able to construct and comprehend.

The Early Hymns' "Jesus" in Opposition to Arius's "Jesus"

In the pre-Arian Christian hymns, the reader noted that those earliest hymns had indeed partially agreed with the Arians in identifying Christ as the Proclaimer, as a human individual, and as the Savior, the one who had accomplished far more for humanity than a human individual could accomplish. The early Christian hymns then candidly and modestly left the identity of Christ veiled in those confessions.

Those hymns demonstrate that the early Christian hymnmakers confessed their belief in Christ with a dialectical faith, whereas the Arians presumed that they had no need for dialectic in their belief.

The First Council of Nicaea—325 C.E.
—Response to Arian Controversy

Running parallel to the ancient Christian river from which the early hymns emerged, there appeared in the fourth century a stream that sprang up from the struggle between the Arians and the believers who confessed Christ as God.

In 324 C.E. Constantine conquered the eastern provinces, where the controversy between the Arians and the orthodox was unsettling civil order. As a response to the unrest, he summoned the first ecumenical council to Nicaea, in the northwest of modern Turkey. Constantine's main interest was to secure civil harmony; he had no concern with theological doctrine apart from its effect on civic order.

The Council attempted to achieve civil harmony by promulgating a universally binding statement of belief, the Nicene Creed. In the creed the bishops defined the teaching regarding Jesus Christ endorsed by the majority of the Council's bishops. They defined Jesus Christ as "of the same substance" as God.

The observer needs to be conscious that, though the majority of bishops were Arian prior to the Council, during the Council they fashioned their doctrine not in terms of their previous belief, but in terms of the belief of the majority of the practicing faithful. The Rule of Faith was observed.

Hymnmakers After Nicaea

There had been a quiet revolution in the church's identification of Jesus Christ.

Thereafter Nicene theology was used to direct the theological stream from which Christian hymns emerged. That is, after the Council of Nicaea there was a major shift in the tone of the belief expressed in the hymns sung to Christ Jesus. There was a significant turning point in the development of the character of Christian hymns. Prior to Nicaea the character of the hymns was poetic and confessional; after Nicaea the character of the hymns became polemically theological.

Because the earliest Christian hymns had been anonymous, they can be interpreted to express not their authors' perspectives, but the belief of the communities that used them in worship.

However after the Council of Nicaea the names of hymnmakers began to emerge. This shift can be interpreted to signify that the hymns after 325 C.E. were no longer expressions of communal belief, but rather of polemical theology in response to the doctrine formulated by the Council of Nicaea.

One such polemical author, Ephrem the Syrian, was a biblical exegete, an ecclesiastical spokesman, a deacon in Syria, and an opponent of the Arians. He lived between approximately 306 and 373. As author of many hymns derived from scripture, he managed to exercise great influence on the later Christian hymns in both Syria and Greece. The belief expressed in his hymns is significant.

His hymn, "The Nicaean," expresses the anti-Arian belief voiced by the Council of Nicaea (325 C.E.); he confessed that Christ "was born from the father before all ages, is God from God, was incarnate from the virgin Mary, and was made man."[9]

Another polemical author of hymns was Hilary of Poitiers (c. 310-66). He lived at approximately the same time as Ephrem the Syrian, a hundred years before the Council of Chalcedon. He wrote several theologically Christian hymns, which insisted that Jesus Christ is God. Unfortunately none of his hymns have survived.

Post-Nicaean Hymns by Ambrose of Milan (340-97 C.E.)

Ambrose was the most significant early hymnmaker whose hymns have been preserved. He flourished in the late fourth century, before the Council of Chalcedon; his hymns championed the theological doctrine that Chalcedon would define; namely, that Christ Jesus is both divine and human.

Aeterne Rerum Conditor
Maker of all, eternal King,
Who day and night about dost bring:
Who weary mortals to relieve
Dost in their times the seasons give.

The herald of the day now resounds,
Always watchful over the depth of
night,
Night's light for the travelers,
Separating one night from the other.
.   .   .   .

Let us thus stand up with courage,
as the cock wakens the players
And alerts those yet asleep,
the cock who drives off those resisting
        day.
.   .   .   .

Jesus, look out to those who totter
And enable us to see;
If you so nourish us, our faults dissolve,
And our sin is resolved in new birth.[10]
(trans. DPL)

Jesus was for Ambrose the Eternal Founder of Things
(Aeterne Rerum Conditor): only the eternal God could be the
eternal founder of things. Moreover, in that hymn Jesus is
praised as ordering the night, the day, and even instincts of
the rooster at dawn. Furthermore he is the one who continues
to nourish humans. This may indeed be a very modest way of
praising God; however it is an explicit confession that Christ
indeed functions as God.

> *Splendor Paterne Gloriae*
>   O Splendor of God's glory bright,
>   O Thou that bringest light from Light,
>   O Light of Light, Light's Living Spring,
>   O Day, all days illumining.[11]

Ambrose here explicitly identifies Christ Jesus as the
"Splendor of God's glory," i.e., as somehow inhering in and
manifesting God's glory.

Hymns to God, the Trinity

Similarly his *Deus Creator Omnium* praises God as
"Maker of all" and "Rule in the height." Ambrose then identifies God and Christ:

> *Deus Creator Omnium*
> To Christ and to the Father now
> And to the Spirit equally,
> We pray for every favoring gift,
> One God Supreme, a Trinity.[12]

The identification of the God as "Trinity" was an extraordinary step, foretelling a doctrine that was just taking form—
the Council of Nicaea, 325 C.E.—as Ambrose was writing.
Ambrose's hymn, *Ecce Jam Noctis* ends with a doxology:

> *Ecce Jam Noctis*
> This let the blessed Deity afford us,
> Father and Son and equal Holy Spirit,
> Whose through the earth be glory in all places
> Ever resounding.[13]

"Father and Son, and equal Holy Spirit" manifests
Ambrose's awareness of the fourth-century Christian belief
that God is three. That vision of God included Christ, the Son
of God, as indeed one in the God who is three. Here Ambrose
took the step from identifying Christ as united with the Father
to acknowledging that in God there is the Father, the Christ,
and another.

Sermo Refectis Artubus similarly ends with a doxology
that identifies Christ, the Son, as the God:

> *Sermo Refectis Artubus*
> Thine Aid, O Loving Father, lend,
> And Son, the Father's Equal, hear,
> With Holy Spirit, Comforter,
> Ruling the ages without end.[14]

There is further evidence of Ambrose's identification of Christ Jesus as "equal" with God.

Hymn to Jesus Christ

Splendor Paternae Gloriae is a hymn to Christ, who brings the light of God to humanity:

> *Splendor Paternae Gloriae*
> O Splendor of God's glory bright,
> O Thou that bringest light from Light,
> O Light of Light, Light's Living Spring,
> O Day, all days illumining.[15]

Christ has come among humanity and brought with him "light from Light," that is, he brought with him divine illumination as a gift for humanity. Only God's "chosen one" could so bring light from Light. Christ is himself the true Light, the Son who is God, but one who is also truly one of the human family.

Here Ambrose moves into a dialectical faith. He confesses that Christ is both human and divine, but does not judge that the human mind needs to resolve the tension between those identities.

The hymn ends, as the previous two, with a doxology to the God who is three: Father, Son, and Holy Paraclete (thus, in this hymn the third in God is identified).

Some hymns, identified as "probable" compositions by Ambrose,[16] name Christ as the God who is able to forgive all human sin. Others, as the one who gives gifts—the gift, for example, which is the glory given to the apostles. Ambrose portrays Christ as having given to the apostles glory from the Father, action by the Son, and the power of will from the Holy Spirit.

Hymns Returning to the Arian Controversy

Prudentius (348–413 C.E.)

The Arian controversy can be dated from 319 to 451 C.E. Prudentius was a Spanish poet and hymn writer who had a civil position as a lawyer. He lived through much of the period of the Arian controversy. During his years of retirement, from approximately 408 to 413 C.E., he wrote anti-Arian hymns. Many of those hymns manifest a reflective, didactic, yet polemical theological argument against the teachings of the Arians. There is value in reading one of these.

Ales Diei Nuntius
(Winged Herald of the Day)
As the bird, whose clarion gay
Sounds before the dawn is gray,
Christ who brings the spirit's day,
Calls us, close at hand:

"Wake!" He cries, "and for my sake,
From your eyes dull slumbers shake!
Sober, righteous, chase, awake!
At the door I stand!"

Lord, to Thee we lift on high
Fervent prayer and bitter cry:
Hearts aroused to pray and sigh
May not slumber more:

Break the sleep of Death and Time,
Forged by Adam's ancient crime;
And the light of Eden's prime
To the world restore!

Unto God the Father, Son,
Holy Spirit, Three in One,
One in Three, be glory done,
Now and evermore.[17]

This is a hymn to the Christ who brings forth the day and to whom the community prays in worship. Christ is also praised as the one who saves humans from "Adam's ancient crime" and who restores to the world "the light of Eden's prime." Thus, Christ has the power to act in a manner in which only God can act. The hymn ends with a doxology.

His *Nox, et Tenebrae, et Nubila* ("Night, and Darkness, and Overcast") praises Christ as the one who removes the shadows from life.

> *Nox, et Tenebrae, et Nubila*
> Day is breaking, dawn is bright:
> Hence, vain shadows of the night!
> Mists that dim our mortal sight,
> Christ is come! Depart!
>
> In Thy beams be purged away
> All that leads our thoughts astray!
> Through our spirits, King of day,
> Pour Thy light divine!

Christ brings his "beams" to purge all heavy thoughts from all humans. Clearly he acts for humans as God. The hymn ends with a doxology.

His *Audit Tyrannus Anxius* ("The Anxious Tyrant Hears") turns to Christ as the one who permits all humans to stand with hope against the temptations of the tyrant.

> *Audit Tyrannus Anxius*
> With terror doth the tyrant hear
> The King of kings hath come to dwell
> Where David's court shall widely rear
> A sceptered reign o'er Israel.
>
> Then cries out, raging, at the word:
> "He comes to stand where we have stood:
> Hence soldier, and with ruthless sword
> Deluge the cradles deep with blood!"

Thus Christ acted for humans as only a divine one can; the divine Christ permits humans to hope in the face of the tempter.

His *O Sola Magnarum Urbium* ("O Sun of the Great Cities") is a Christmas hymn that praises Bethlehem.

> *O Sola Magnarum Urbium*
> Bethlehem! of noblest cities
> None can once with thee compare;
> Thou alone the Lord from heaven
> Didst for us incarnate bear.
>
> Fairer than the sun at morning
> Was the star that told His birth;
> To the lands their God announcing
> Hid beneath a form of earth.

There the Incarnate one was born; there he became a human. Yet he is also praised here as "the Lord from heaven," whose birth as a human enabled God to hide the divine presence in a lowly form here on earth. Christ, whether a superhuman person, as Arius contended, or as a human individual who is God, as the church tensively confessed, made God present to the world of humanity. The hymn ends with a doxology.

His *Quicumque Christum Quaeritis* ("You Who Seek Christ") is a hymn to Christ on high, seated as the God with the Father.

> *Quicumque Christum Quaeritis*
> All ye who would the Christ descry,
> Lift up your eyes to Him on high:
> There mortal gaze hath strength to see
> The token of His majesty.
>
> A wondrous sign we there behold,
> That knows not death nor groweth old

> Sublime, most high, that cannot fade,
> That was ere earth and heaven were made.
>
> Here is the King the Gentiles fear,
> The Jews' most mighty King is here
> Promised to Abraham of yore,
> And to his seed forevermore.

Christ is the King, foretold by the prophets. Thus, Christ is the agent from God who has visited humanity as the person whom God had sent.

Finally his *Salvete, Flores Martyrum* ("Hail, Blooms of Martyrs") sings first to the holy innocents, killed by Herod in his attempt to kill the infant Jesus.

> *Salvete, Flores Martyrum*
> All hail! ye infant martyr flowers,
> Cut off in life's first dawning hours:
> As rosebuds snapt in tempest strife,
> When Herod sought your Savior's life.
>
> You, tender flock of lambs, we sing,
> First victims slain for Christ your King:
> Beside the very altar, gay
> With palms and crowns, ye seem to play.
>
> All honor, laud, and glory be,
> O Jesu, virgin-born to Thee;
> All glory, as is ever meet,
> To Father and to Paraclete.

The hymn then praises Jesus both as the elevated, divine King and as the lowly, human infant born of the virgin.

The hymns praise Christ with a belief that confesses him as an individual shrouded from human comprehension: he is the human being whom reason can acknowledge; yet, he is also somehow a divine representative whom only the stretch of imaginative belief can confess.

Church Response to the Continued Arian Controversy

In the form of a creed, the Nicene Creed, the church condemned the Arian doctrine at the Council of Nicaea (325 C.E.), which confessed Christ as having the same substance as God and as being God from God.

However the Arian doctrine, after a period of decline in the first years after the Council of Nicaea, then revived throughout the Mediterranean world.

The Council of Chalcedon convened in 451 in order to again condemn Arius's doctrine and to resolve the tension between the churches in Alexandria and Antioch regarding Christ's identity.

After Chalcedon's definition of Christ as fully human and fully divine, the pre-Nicaean tradition of devout and theologically tentative hymns seems to have died out, as the post-Nicaean tradition of theologically polemical hymns regarding Christ became the norm. The post-Chalcedonian hymn in the Christian liturgies makes theologically confrontational statements in order to press upon the community of believers the ecclesiastical opposition to Arius. That opposition took the form of insisting that Christ Jesus was not only Savior, Son of God, and Messiah, as Arius had asserted, but was also God, which Arius had denied.

Post-Chalcedonian Hymns: Anatolius, a Fifth-Century Greek Hymn Writer

Anatolius (d. 458 C.E.) wrote short and polemical theological, anti-Arian hymns. Anatolius , one of the bishops at Chalcedon who had formulated the identification of Christ Jesus as fully man and fully God, authored approximately one hundred hymns. His hymns proclaim the Chalcedonian theology that Christ is man and God. Only a few of those hymns bear study here.

First, his *Evening Hymn:*

> *Evening Hymn*
> The day is past and over!
> All thanks, O Lord, to Thee!
> I pray thee now that sinless
> The eve and night may be
> Grant that I crave, O God, and save!
>
> . . . .
>
> Lighten mine eyes, O Savior!
> Or sleep in death shall I;
> And he, mine adversary,
> Triumphantly shall cry
> I have assailed and have prevailed.
>
> Be Thou my soul's preserver!
> O God! for Thou dost know
> The snares and sins are many
> Through which I have to go
> Lover of men, oh hear my call,
> And guard and save me from them all.

Anatolius here praises Christ Jesus as "O God"—imaginative belief. However he then also identifies him as one who knows all temptations that humans must endure, a human individual, as "my soul's preserver," as "Lover of men," as One who is capable of saving each human from all the perils of life.

These might appear to twentieth-century believers as traditional symbols of belief in Christ. However in the fifth century such proclamations confronted the Arians who refused to identify Christ as God with the official and inflammatory Chalcedonian belief.

Next his *St. Stephen's Day—Stichera at Vespers*

> *St. Stephen's Day—Stichera at Vespers*
> The Lord and King of all things

> Upon the earth is born.
> The Lord and King of all
> things
> But yesterday was born.

Anatolius identifies the one who "yesterday was born," Christ Jesus, as "the Lord and King of all things." Such an identification of Jesus is a reserved manner of proclaiming him to be the representative of God among humans. Praise of Christ as the one who is able to atone for human sins is a praise that could be given only to one who is able to exercise the divine capacity to forgive and to remit human sins. Anatolius again aims directly at the facade of the Arian embattlements.

There are too many hymns by Anatolius to consider each of them. However the themes that he develops deserve to be identified.

Anatolius's *Stichera for a Sunday of the First Tone* explicitly identifies the Christ in the boat during the storm on the lake (Mt 8:18-27) as "the God of God," "the Light of Light," and "Truth of Truth." Such identifications would have confronted the Arians aggressively because the hymns proclaim Christ Jesus as not only the great human, but also as God.

Anatolius's *Stichera for Christmastide* insists that Jesus was the Word made flesh, God, at whose birth the angels sang, the Monarch, the Savior, and the Lord. Thus the Christ is unequivocally God; Christ bears the identity that the Arians refused to attribute to him.

His *Idiolelon for Christmas* identifies even the infant who was born at Bethlehem as the everlasting God who is Savior. The Arians insisted, regarding the Son or the *Logos,* that "there was when he was not," that the Son was begotten before the beginning of time from God and thus could not be God. Jesus, the Son, born again and therefore having a beginning in time, could not be the everlasting God. Neither the Son nor the Christ could be the eternal God. Yet for Anatolius, reflecting at

Christmas on the incarnation, there had *not* been a time when he was not.

Anatolius praised him whom Mary's womb contained as the One who is unable to be contained. He who came in human birth brought with him from his previous state the fullness of his everlasting love, the love that he could only have brought from the God.

Other Post-Chalcedonian Hymns

Ambrosian Hymns (fifth and sixth centuries)

Ambrose (340-97 C.E.), bishop of Milan between 374 and 397, was the inspiration from whom the Ambrosian Rite emerged. That rite observes a distinct liturgical cycle of feasts, as well as a distinct liturgical celebration of the Eucharist. Ambrose himself was a dominant influence on the hymns and psalmody that spread out from Milan. Such is the claim made by his protégé, Augustine of Hippo, and his assistant and biographer, Paul the Deacon.[18] Both Ambrosian theology and his favored chant style motivated a great many hymns that continued to appear even in the two centuries after his death. Thus one who studies the Ambrosian hymns needs to situate them within the interrelationship between the theologies of Ambrose and those of the Arians. That confrontation of theologies had begun before Ambrose died, but continued long after his passing.

There is a style of religious hymnody known as Ambrosian. There are far too many such hymns to permit even a cursory study of them here. However the Christology of those hymns can be synthesized by reflecting upon a very few examples.

The *Aurora Caelum Purpurat* is a fourth-or fifth-century Ambrosian hymn in celebration of Easter.

Aurora Caelum Purpurat
The morn had spread her crimson rays,
When rang the skies with shouts of praise;
Earth joined the joyful hymn to swell,
That brought despair to vanquished hell.

He comes victorious from the grave,
The Lord omnipotent to save,
And brings with Him to light of day
The Saints who long imprisoned lay.[19]

This is a hymn to Christ, "the Lord omnipotent," who saved all humans from death. The sign that he was capable of achieving that universal salvation was that death could not conquer him: rather he had conquered death. Therefore he is the mirror of the divine one, who lives, no more to die.

The *Tristes Erant Apostoli* is also a fourth-or fifth-century Ambrosian Easter hymn.

Tristes Erant Apostoli
While Christ's disciples grieving sad,
Their Master's painful death deplore,
Whom faithless servants' cruel hands
Had bathed in his own crimson gore.
Quick from the happy realms above,
An Angel comes on joyful wing,
And to the women tells the joy
That to His flock their Lord will bring.

. . . .

That Thou mayst be our Paschal joy
Through happy, never-ending years,
Thine own poor children, Jesu, free
From sin's sad death with all its fears.[20]

This is a reflection upon the apostles, whose master, Christ, had indeed died: he thus had been a full human mortal. Yet that same master appeared to his disciples after his death: he thus was the conqueror of death, the one who lives forever with the Father. Thus, he was somehow—a dialectical belief—one who is superior to the termination of death at the same time that he was human.

The *Paschale Mundo Gaudium* is an Ambrosian Easter hymn from the fourth or fifth century.

> *Paschale Mundo Gaudium*
> With the fair sun of Easter morn
> The world's excelling joy is born,
> When, bright with new and greater grace,
> The Apostles see the Savior's face.
>
> They in their Lord's fair flesh descry
> The wounds that shine as stars on high,
> And, wondering, faithful witness bear,
> And all that they have seen declare.
>
> O Christ, most loving King, we pray,
> Possess our inmost hearts today,
> While grateful lips with glad acclaim
> Sing fervent praises to Thy Name.[21]

The Christ who was seen by the apostles on Easter was clothed in his wounds, that is, he was experienced as the human one who had suffered death. However he was then known as the risen Christ who had conquered death. As such he is imaginatively confessed as our Easter joy eternally—the uniquely Chosen One. The Risen One was able to challenge all to trust that their human existence extends beyond the limit of death, and continues to challenge them to trust that they are freed from death's power, that they might live to be with God.

The *Aeterne Rex Altissime* is an Ambrosian hymn of the fifth century.

> *Aeterne Rex Altissime*
> Eternal Monarch, King most High,
> Whose blood hath brought redemption nigh,

By whom the death of Death was wrought,
And conquering grace's battle fought:

Ascending by the starry road,
This day Thou wentest home to God,
By Heaven to power unending called,
And by no human hand installed.

That so, in nature's triple frame,
Each heavenly and each earthly name,
And things in hell's abyss abhorred,
May bend the knee and own Him Lord.[22]

This is praise to Christ, the human King most high, who suffered death, but who as the Divine One conquered death and won thereby salvation for all humans. Moreover Christ then "went home to God." Therefore the human destiny of all of humanity, since all have been joined with him, has been changed—only God's uniquely Chosen One could have so transformed the whole of humanity. Moreover the divine Christ purges all sins away and draws all hearts by grace to heaven. Christ is known not only as the man who died, but is also believed to be death's unique Conqueror, who reigns yet as King. As such a One, he receives homage from every knee.

The *Deus Tuorum Militum* raises the hearts of the community to the divine Christ.

Deus Tuorum Militum
God, Choice and Crown of your own soldiers

. . . .

Here certainly you are the world's joy,
The food, replacing empty pomp,
You forswore the sated lures
And attained heaven.

He lived as a human in the midst of "sin and the pomp of sin," but forswore those lures. Though he was the divinely

Chosen One, he endured the torments of living as a human in the midst of sin—again the tensive confession of imaginative belief in Christ as God and the rational acknowledgment that he was human. Still as God, he remained apart from sin. The hymn ends with a doxology.

The *Christo Profusum Sanguinem* identifies Christ as the one for whom the martyrs died.

> *Christo Profusum Sanguinem*
> The Martyrs' triumphs let us sing,
> Their blood poured forth for Christ the King,
> And while due hymns of praise we pay,
> Our thankful hearts cast grief away.
>
> The world its terrors urged in vain;
> They recked not of the body's pain;
> One step, and holy death made sure
> The life that ever shall endure.
>
> . . . .
>
> Redeemer, hear us of Thy love,
> That with the Martyr host above,
> Hereafter, of Thine endless grace,
> Thy servants also may have place.[23]

Christ was judged by the martyrs to be one who is worthy of absolute commitment. They regarded him as God's Chosen One. The hymn also identifies him as the Redeemer: a dialectical belief.

The *Jesu, Corona Virginum* also worships Jesus as the one worthy of absolute commitment.

> *Jesu, Corona Virginum*
> Jesu, the Virgins' crown, do Thou
> Accept us as in prayer we bow;
> Born of that Virgin, whom alone
> The Mother and the Maid we own.
>
> . . . .

> We pray Thee therefore to bestow
> Upon our senses here below
> Thy grace, that so we may endure
> From taint of all corruption pure.[24]

Yet this hymn also worships Jesus as one who, in being born of Mary, entered the human community—the tensive acknowledgment of Jesus as a human. The hymn ends with a doxology.

The *Jam Christus Astra Ascenderat* identifies Christ as having ascended to the place from which he came; just as he came from God, so he returned to God.

> *Jam Christus Astra Ascenderat*
> Now Christ had passed the starry host,
> Returned to Heaven, to highest place,
> Whence He will send the Holy Ghost
> To comfort, by the Father's grace.

Clearly he is thus united with God. It focuses upon Christ as having sent the rush of flames upon the apostles at Pentecost, which was evidence of Christ's unity with the God.

The *Aeterna Caeli Gloria* was a fifth-century hymn in Ambrosian chant that prays to Christ, who is both the son of Mary and the Son of the Highest.

> *Aeterna Caeli Gloria*
> Eternal glory of high heaven,
> Blessed hope dispelling mortal gloom,
> God's Only Son unto us given,
> Fruit of the holy Virgin's womb.
>
> Give aid to us who rise anew,
> Our souls in calm resolve upraise,
> To pay Thee grateful homage due,
> From hearts that glow in God's high praise.

He is the one who renews and sanctifies every human life with joyous hope, strong faith, and charity. Therefore he is the one whom God uniquely chose to act for God among humans.

The *Ad Regias Angi Dapes* is a sixth-century Ambrosian hymn that praises Christ, our Lamb and King.

> *Ad Regias Angi Dapes*
> Now, bidden to the Lamb's high feast,
> In fairest robes let's meet his eyes,
> The Red Sea of our bondage passed,
> Let song to Christ, our Leader, rise.
>
> Whose charity, divinely great,
> Gives us to drink His Sacred Blood,
> Whose love, high priest, doth immolate
> His Blessed Flesh to be our food.

As Lamb he is the human one who suffered the crucifixion, the piercing with the lance, and death. As King he reigns as the God's chosen Priest and gives his blood as wine to his followers. He is "Mighty Victim from the sky," both God's Chosen One and a human: a tensive belief.

The *Rex Sempiterne Caelitum* is also a sixth-century Ambrosian hymn that praises Christ the King.

> *Rex Sempiterne Caelitum*
> O Thou, the heavens' eternal King,
> Creator, unto Thee we sing,
> With God the Father ever One,
> Coequal, coeternal Son.
>
> Thy hand, when first the world began,
> Made in Thine own pure image man,
> And yoked to fleshly form of earth
> A living form of heavenly birth.
>
> And when the envy of the foe
> Had marred Thy noblest work below,

Clothed in our flesh, Thou didst restore
The image Thou hadst made before.

Once wast Thou born of Mary's womb;
And now, newborn from out the tomb,
O Christ, Thou bidd'st us rise with Thee
From death to immortality.[25]

Christ here is Creator, "with God coequal and coeternal Son." Yet he was also tensively "clothed in our flesh" and thus capable of acting in our place to restore the human race whom indeed he had made at the dawn of time. Thus, not only was Jesus born from Mary's womb as a human, but he was also newborn from the tomb as the eternal Shepherd, as the One who had acted for God.

Post-Ambrosian Hymns to Christ

In the late sixth century the Greek hymn, *Stauro Theotokion,* emerged in the Christian liturgies of the church.

Stauro Theotokion sings to the Christ who had been unjustly "slaughtered," to the one who "innocently suffered." Thus, he is praised as a human being. Yet in a tensive confession it also sings to him as one who was able to unite the whole world with his sacrifice: it praises him as the One who had been able to unite the world with God because he is united with God. No mere human would have so been able to focus the entire world's vulnerability to death within his own sufferings. Moreover it turns to Christ as to one who can respond to an appeal for the mercy that is needed by sinners; only God could offer such mercy.

Stauro Theotokion
O Christ, in mourning for you, her innocent son,
The sorrowful Virgin regards you crucified and sighs:
"Child most sweet, how unjustly you suffer!

> How you are crucified there on the tree!
> How the whole earth is crucified on you!
> Do not abandon me, your mother and servant,
> Who beseeches you, O merciful benefactor."
>
>   (trans. DPL)

This brief sermon-hymn is addressed to Christ, who suffered grievously, innocently, and lovingly—thus humanly. Yet "the whole earth is crucified on you," that is, the sufferings due to all the earth fell upon this One whom God had chosen as the One uniquely capable of resolving the penal sufferings due to "the whole earth."

A century later the Greek hymn, *Apolutikia,* a sermon in verse, emerged in the liturgies of the church.

> *Apolutikia*
> Christ rose from the dead,
> Having trodden death to nought,
> Having granted life to
> Those gripped by death.
>
> Christ has risen from the dead,
> Death to naught hath down he trod;
> And on those within the tombs
> Life he hath bestowed.
>
>   (trans. DPL)

Apolutikia thus addresses Christ, risen from the dead, who conquered death and bestowed life upon all who live in death's shadow. Because Christ was able to overcome death by dying, a divine force was active within him.

In this hymn Christ is the unique human who rose from the dead and thus liberated all humans from death. Thus he is both human in that he died and much more than human in that he destroyed the power of death and granted immortality to all.

In St. Cosmos's Canon for Christmas Day (eighth century) there appeared the Greek hymn, *Christos Gennatae, Doxsasate.*

Christos Gennatae, Doxsasate
Christ is born. Shout forth his fame.
Christ, born human. Reckn'd as us.
Christ, born on earth. 'Counter him here
Sing to the Lord, O all the earth.
(trans. DPL)

Christos Gennatae is a Greek hymn addressed to Christ, who on the one hand is born as a human and lived on earth, but who on the other hand is descended from heaven. He is both the human son of Mary and the Lord to whom all humans turn in hope. He is a human individual, but also one in whom others found evidence that God dwells among humans.

The poet who composed this eighth-century hymn envisioned Christ as in that age remaining present to the community, who were able still to encounter Christ among them— "'Counter him here." Thus he is categorically different from any other human who had lived.

Post-Chalcedonian Tradition of Christology in Hymns

The tradition of using hymns to encourage orthodox belief continued into the following centuries. Hymns were encouraged by the church in its effort to form the belief of the community according to the Christology of Chalcedon. The tone of hymns used by the believing community shifted from that of relatively spontaneous, communal expressions to the color of didactic lessons in Chalcedonian theology.

Prior to the Council of Nicaea the hymns had indeed appeared to embody expressions that might have had their origins in a response to the Spirit who moved in the consciousness of the community of believers.

However after the Council of Nicaea and again after that of Chalcedon, the tone of the hymns used by the community shifted to polemical, theological insistence upon the doctrine that the church at Nicaea and Chalcedon had approved. The bishops who supported the doctrine of those two councils had perhaps assumed the office of commissioning didactic hymns for communal worship. One who reads those hymns and reflects upon them might well perceive them as more representative of polemical theology and less expressive of a praying community's trusting belief in Jesus, the Good Shepherd. These cerebrally articulated words of praise lost the color of inspired words; they had become reasoned, theological arguments.

These early hymns did, however, continue to articulate the dialectical tension that needed to be maintained in identifying the Christ of faith.

There are again far too many such hymns to present here, but a random sampling of them reveals the continued expression of the tensive faith in Christ Jesus' identity.

The *Te Deum* is a Latin hymn from the late fourth or early fifth centuries.

Te Deum

O God, we praise you,
As Lord we confess you.
Eternal Father, all the earth reveres you.
The angels, the heavens and all the powers,
The cherubim and seraphim unceasingly proclaim:
Holy, holy, holy is the Lord God of hosts.
Heaven and earth are full
Of your majesty and glory.

.   .   .   .

You are a glorious King, O Christ,
The Father's eternal Son;
Yet at your coming to take upon you
The human nature that you would release,
A virgin's womb had no dismay for you.
Drawing death's sting,
You opened the kingdom of heaven

To all who would believe.
You sit at God's right hand,
Sharing the Father's glory;
And we believe that you will come and judge us.[26]

This hymn, addressed to the God, the Father, identified the Son with the Father. Christ is addressed in the hymn (one must recall that the hymn is addressed to the God, the Father) as the King of glory, the "eternal" son of the Father. Yet that same Christ is addressed as he who took human nature, even to the point of assuming fragile life within the virgin's womb. Nonetheless that same human Christ will act as the divinely chosen judge of all humanity: the hymn identifies him tensively as the one who acts for the God. Finally the hymn identifies Christ as the Redeemer who makes his servants to be with the saints in glory forever. Christ is thus both a human individual and the divinely appointed agent of God.

A *Solis Ortus Cardine* is a fifth-century Latin hymn by Sedulius. It sings to Christ, who is "virgin-born, the Son of Mary, Christ the King," who has "this earthly frame," "a servant's form," who therefore was able to act as a human to represent all humans in "liberating flesh by flesh." Nonetheless he who was formed as human in Mary's womb was formed as well by divine grace. Thus the one incarnate Christ was formed both as the human son of Mary and as the one whom God had selected to be the divinely appointed agent among humans. That tension between identifying Christ as a human individual and as the divine agent among humans was expressed by a series of contrasting images within the hymn. It concludes with a doxology.

Crudelis Herodes, Deum, which is also by Sedulius, repeats that dialectical tension.

> *Crudelis Herodes, Deum*
> Why, impious Herod, vainly fear
> That Christ the Savior cometh here?

He takes no earthly realms away
Who gives the crown that lasts for aye.

. . . .

In holy Jordan's purest wave
The heavenly Lamb vouchsafed to lave;
That he, to whom was sin unknown,
Might cleanse his people from their own.

. . . .

Jesus to thee be glory meet,
Who shinest o'er earth in light and love,
So to the Sire and Paraclete
Let earth resound and heaven above.[27]

The infant who was born during the reign of Herod the Great was "The heavenly Lamb" who knew no sin. Though human, he was sinless. As divine, he was to cleanse his people from their sins. Moreover he turned water into wine. Nevertheless he had begun his human life just as any human. The tension between the human and the divine in Christ is acute in this hymn.

Victimae Paschali was written perhaps in Germany in 1199.

Victimae Paschali
Christ the Lord is risen today;
Christians, haste your vows to pay;
Offer ye your praises meet
At the Paschal Victim's feet;

For the sheep the Lamb hath bled,
Sinless in the sinner's stead.
Christ the Lord is risen on high;
Now he lives, no more to die.

Christ the Victim undefiled,
Man to God hath reconciled;
When in strange and awful strife
Met together Death and Life.[28]

This is the Easter Sequence. Christ is praised as the paschal victim, the lamb who as human was slaughtered for the sins of the sheep: he suffered as only a human is able to suffer. However he is also "Christ the Lord, risen on high; now he lives, no more to die."

Résumé of the Historical Study of Belief as Expressed in Hymns

After having brushed lightly across the history of the belief of the early Christian hymns, we might well reflect upon the belief or beliefs that such a cursory glance at early Christian history has revealed.

There is expressed in the early hymns a series of beliefs in Christ. Those beliefs are presented in hymns that emerged from the very beginning of belief in Christ and from the succeeding centuries through to the twelfth century.

Apparently Christians over that entire span of time spontaneously and continuously believed in Christ tensively.

Thus by the Rule of Faith one can conclude that the Spirit has been directing the community of believers since the beginning to confess their belief in Christ with a tension between Christ known as human and Christ imaginatively believed as the Son whom God had sent to act among humans in God's place.

The Hymns' Tensive Confession of Christ

Thus there are many hymns that insist that Christ can be identified, neither as a human, nor as a god, but only as one who exists in a tension between his identity as a human and his identity as the Chosen One of God.

The earliest hymns, such as Philippians 2:6-11, reveal that the believing community had been praising Christ Jesus as both

God and human from the beginning. The belief of the community had thus from the very beginning, from about 55 C.E., the date of Philippians, viewed Christ Jesus as one who could be identified only in tension between Christ as human and Christ as divine. That was the kind of dialectical tension in his identity that the Council of Chalcedon after four centuries of Christianity was to confess as the orthodox doctrine in 451 C.E.

So too the hymn in 1 Peter 2:22-25 approaches Christ Jesus dialectically. The believing community identified him both as their brother, as a human being who struggled successfully with sin and suffering, and as one who is far more than their brother, as one able to achieve salvation for the entire human community.

Again, the author of the hymn in 1 Timothy 3:16 concurred with the authors of the previous hymns in identifying Christ Jesus dialectically. Neither the category of the human nor that of the divine was adequate to describe the One to whom believers confessed their fidelity.

The hymn in John 1:1-14 does not attempt to identify Christ as belonging univocally to one category. While the author avoids categorizing him, the hymn chooses to leave the identification of Christ shaded in ambiguity.

The author of the hymn *Phos Hilaron* imaged Christ's identity in a form that harmonized with the previously cited early hymns. The *Phos Hilaron* also insists that, though Christ is certainly human, he is far more elevated and powerful than any merely human person could be.

Obviously this hymnmaker concurred that Christ was not to be categorized within one of those neat definitions with which the human mind defines experiences. Rather this author followed the previous authors in portraying Christ as one whose identity is far more complex than the human mind can grasp.

In its final stanza the *Phos Hilaron* introduces the doxology of Father, Son, and Spirit, implying that Christ shares a unity with God that is more intimate than the unity that might be claimed for a human redeemer. With that final stanza the author took a definite step toward identifying Christ Jesus as one with the God.

Nevertheless the manner in which the Son, together with the Father and the Spirit, might be the God was neither the problem nor the concern of the author. That interrelationship would only become the problem and the intellectual concern of those who were conscious that the identification of God as three was an enigma that deserved a resolution. However a step toward the awareness of that problem was taken in this hymn. Eventually believers would become conscious that the three in God would require that such a plurality must be elaborated into a unity.

The *Phos Hilaron* aligned itself with the prior hymns in its identification of Christ in a dialectical tension between Christ as human and the Christ as divine. The author of this hymn, as those of the prior hymns, was not interested in moving beyond that dialectical tension, but was content to leave Christ situated somewhere between the human and the divine dimensions.

The hymnmaker of *Bridle of Steeds Untamed* was another author who identified Christ as one who was far more than one who was simply human, as one who somehow participated in the "royal" bloodline of God. However the author did not presume to be able to reduce Christ to any intellectual categories that the human mind had devised.

So too the *Odes of Solomon* confessed that, as elevated and sublime as Christ the Redeemer is, he is not to be reduced to a logical category of man or of God. On the contrary the author of the *Odes* chose to leave the precise identification of the Christ unexpressed. He appears to have been content to conclude that a Redeemer as elevated as the Christ was one who has an identity that the human mind is not able to determine rationally.

Jesus is understood in the *Odes* as capable of proclaiming with his word a unique knowledge of the Most High. The hymn writer believed Christ had foreknowledge of his followers before they were born. Both of those assertions (*Ode* 8) identified Jesus as the unique one: he not only knows God intimately (he proclaims the human knowledge of God), but also shares in the knowledge of God (from the divine perspective he knew the identity of his disciples before they were born). Because Christ shared so intimately with God, he consequently can be identified as uniquely related to God. Yet how he is identified, in what categories can humans place him, is unexpressed, perhaps unknowable.

In the *Odes* the Christ is portrayed in highly inflated images. The author used such images to insist that believers are to consider their Lord not simply as a unique human individual, nor simply as Savior, nor as any other comprehensible substance, but as the one who possessed an awareness that was beyond the range of what the human mind can grasp. Christ is indeed human, but also is one who eludes the categories that humans have available to them to identify what they know. Thus those in the worshiping community discovered that their faith in Christ had so developed that they confessed him to be somehow more conscious of God than any human could be. They identified him as somehow in union with God in a way that others could not be.

V. The Early Church's Declarations about Christ in Its Hymns

Having considered the belief expressed in the earliest Christian communities' hymns, we can ask to what degree the official church formulated its doctrine according to the hymns about Christ. If there is a relationship between church doctrine and the early hymns, then the church attempted to be faithful to belief as revealed by the Holy Spirit in those early hymns.

Letter to the Ephesians—Approval of Spontaneous Belief

The Letter to the Ephesians (c. 80 C.E.) suggests a very early effort by a Christian community to impose a degree of discipline upon those who chose to worship spontaneously:

> [15] Look carefully then how you walk, not as unwise men but as wise, [16] making the most of the time, because the days are evil. [17] Therefore do not be foolish, but understand what the will of the Lord is. [18] And do not get drunk with wine, for that is debauchery; but be filled with the Spirit, [19] addressing one another in psalms and hymns and spiritual songs, singing and making melody to the Lord with all your heart, [20] always and for everything giving

thanks in the name of our Lord Jesus Christ to God the
Father. (Eph 5:15-20)

The author was approving of individuals' spontaneous
responses in worship ("be filled with the Spirit, addressing
one another..."). However he insisted that individuals were to
discipline themselves in their responses ("do not get drunk
with wine....") and to learn to be sensitive to their inner spirit;
namely, to *the* Spirit. Thus, if they felt impelled to sing out,
they were to honor that impulse as given to them by the
Spirit.

Apparently those very early vocal expressions ("addressing one another in psalms....") were imaginatively believed to
be religious responses to the numinous Spirit, present within
the members of the community. On the one hand believers
who came from the Hebrew tradition would likely have
expressed themselves in the cadences that the Jews used in
their singing of the psalms. On the other hand those who
came from the Greek tradition would likely have expressed
themselves in more freely charismatic forms of hymns, such
as the Greeks used in their temple worship of Apollo and in
their theater performances.

With both Hebrew and Greek Christians the author
insists that spontaneous worship is to emerge from the inner
life of the individuals ("but be filled with the Spirit, addressing one another..."). This implies that the earliest Christians
were challenged to revere their interior feelings during worship by fashioning charismatic hymns.[1]

Development of Specifically Christian Hymns

From that early challenge the Christian community of
believers began to form distinctively Christian hymns. Though
the first Christian pattern of worship was to use Hebrew psalms
for worship, increasingly the Hellenic Christian community

shifted away from the use of Hebrew psalms and toward Hellenic hymns written by Christians whom the Hellenic muse inspired. At the very least one might say that they shifted toward music composed by Greek Christians, rather than by Hebrews.

Fragments of such hymns appear in various books of the New Testament:

> *First Letter to Timothy*
> [16] He was manifested in the flesh,
> vindicated in the Spirit,
> seen by angels,
> preached among the nations,
> believed on in the world,
> taken up in glory (1 Tim 3:16)

> *Second Letter to Timothy*
> [11] If we have died with him,
> we shall also live with him;
> [12] if we endure, we shall also reign with him;
> if we deny him, he also will deny us;
> [13] if we are faithless, he remains faithful—
> for he cannot deny himself. (2 Tim 2:11)

Apparently individuals within the Christian community were not inspired to compose these hymns according to the model of the Hebrew psalms, nor by the example of Hellenic drama. They believed that the interior Spirit gave birth to the belief-in-Christ of the members of the Christian communities. The rhythmic repetition and pulse of the hymns quoted here suggest that they emerged first from spokesmen, speaking in tongues, and then from prophets, interpreting the charism.

Increasing Importance of Christian Hymns

As congregational song became the characteristic manner in which believers manifested the life of the Spirit, hymns replaced the gift of tongues as the standard expression of Christian belief. As the author of the Letter to the Ephesians insisted, worship was not to be done any longer "in empty words," which are appropriate for those who are in "darkness" (Eph 5: 6–8). Rather those who were in "the light" were challenged to express the Spirit "in psalms and hymns and spiritual songs, singing and making melody to the Lord with all your heart" (Eph 5: 19). The author of the Letter to the Ephesians in approximately 80 c.e. was urging the Christian community at Ephesus to formulate a new manner of expressing joy in Christ. No longer were they to rely only upon the gift of tongues, nor even upon the interpretation of tongues as appropriate for Christian worship of the Lord.

Paul's first letter to the Corinthians (c. 54 c.e.) expresses that modification in his evaluation of charismatic gifts:

> [14]For if I pray in a tongue, my spirit prays but my mind is unfruitful. [15] What am I to do? I will pray with the spirit and I will pray with the mind also; I will sing with the spirit and I will sing with the mind also (1 Cor. 14: 14-15).

So the worshiping community began to focus deliberately upon the composition of hymns as its appropriate manner of expressing the joy of belief. New hymns, which were not specifically Christian, emerged; these were intended to express the enthusiasm that had not been expressed in the music that had been borrowed from Hebrew and Hellenic music.[2]

Christian Belief Expressed in Christian Hymnody

By the end of the first century the music that was being used in Christian worship used metric rhythms—beauty that seemed to be spontaneous joy. The strict limits of Hebrew and Hellenic meters gave way to a form of plainchant, more spontaneous and free than the pre-Christian musical traditions.[3]

That music gradually came to be a convention. Then Justin Martyr (c. 100-65 C.E.) recognized the need to rejuvenate the music of Christian worship. He proposed that the music of worship might imitate the music of folk culture, in order to express the joy of Christian belief.

The same approval of the vernacular music of the folk culture is found in the writings of Clement of Alexandria as the third century began.

After Constantine's Edict of Milan in 313 C.E., Christian music took on its form of plainchant that would include Ambrosian, Sarum, Armenian, Byzantine, Coptic, Syrian, Gallican, and Mozarabic traditions. These various forms of plainchant seem to the modern ear to be less than spontaneous; however they establish a serene atmosphere of prayerful worship within the community gathered for liturgical action.[4]

Thus, when Ambrose, bishop of Milan (374-97 C.E.), desired to promote greater joy in the worship of the believing community, he urged the development of antiphonal singing in worship. Thereafter the typical Christian form of sung worship was a hymnic dialogue within the community. For example, in response to the priest's conclusion of the sung eucharistic prayer, the community could sing the "Amen." The priest and the congregation sang the "Kyrie Eleison" antiphonally. The community similarly responded musically to the priest's various sung addresses to the community. Thus in response to the priest's address, "the Lord be with you," the community would sing "and with your spirit." This form of worship in dialogue was intended to express the joy that the Spirit was inspiring within the Christian community.[5]

Increasingly the music of Christian worship became plainchant, since the community preferred that musical expression of the freedom that the Spirit inspired in their belief and worship. Hymn singing that was not in plainchant did not cease entirely; thereafter it remained on the margin of the western church's liturgical music.

Polemics in Christian Hymnody

When the church fashioned a deliberate response to the Arians, who maintained their heterodoxy from about 320 to 460 C.E., church music underwent another change. This second change was quite different from the earlier change from Hebrew and Greek chant to the free and spontaneous plainchant. The anti-Arian modification transformed church music from the charismatic expression of communal belief to the expression of anti-Arian polemics. Prior to that transformation the church had fashioned its music to articulate interior devotion. However because of the rational appeal of his theology, Arius had introduced a major Christological crisis that disrupted the church of the fourth century. Thus church music took on a new purpose: to articulate doctrine that the bishops claimed the Spirit had inspired in opposition to the Arian teachings.

Arius convinced many believers at Antioch and throughout the East that Jesus may indeed be the Savior, the Word of God, and even the Son of God, yet *not* God. He argued most persuasively that Jesus could not have been God since "there was when he was not." As conventional orthodoxy taught, the Son of God had been begotten by the Father; therefore he had a beginning. Since he had a beginning and since God had no beginning, Jesus could not, therefore, be identified unequivocally with God. Rather he must be identified with those who are creatures. He had not always been, as the eternal God has always been; thus the Son of God is limited, while God has no limit.

The church in Rome rejected Arius's interpretation of the relationship between Christ and God as too restricted by the limitations of human reasoning. The Roman Church insisted that believers were to confess that Jesus Christ was not only a human individual, but also God, just as the Father is God.

It was for the purpose of clarifying and defining this

issue that the Council of Nicaea (325 c.e.) was summoned by the Emperor Constantine. Constantine needed to resolve the religious controversy about Christ and God that was creating civil unrest within the empires.

The Council assembled at Nicaea in Bithynia (now Iznik in contemporary Turkey), where they would be under the watchful care of Emperor Constantine at Constantinople (modern Istanbul). The extraordinary interest of the emperor in the definition of the identity of Christ was based upon his concern that there needed to be religious unity within the entire empire if there was to be civil unity. He hoped to insure that the religious divisiveness concerning the identity of Christ would cease and that strife would be replaced by political order. He intended to direct the fathers assembled close to his throne to draw up a definition that would result in peace.

Growing Attraction of Arian Faith

However the religious strife caused by the Arians was much more than a consequence of popular, religious piety. The debate between the followers of Arius's doctrine and the adherents of the Roman church's doctrine also involved a demand by the regional bishops, especially those aligned with Antioch and Alexandria, for decentralized doctrinal authority. Regional bishops were insisting upon their own autonomous ecclesiastical authority; they resented the centralized authority that the Roman ecclesiastical hierarchy claimed. By the time that Arius began to preach and Constantine began to reign, discontent had developed among many regional bishops within the centralized rule of the church in Rome. Regionalism developed throughout the non-Roman communities in the empire: each region and its bishop insisted upon its right to govern itself and to determine its own doctrine.[6]

Thus many believers outside of Rome aligned themselves with Arianism, not so much to oppose the Christology that the church in Rome endorsed, but to state that they were no longer willing to be ruled by a foreign and distant centralized church. They intended to oppose not so much the orthodoxy of the church in Rome, but the political power of that church, which had come to be identified in their minds with the emperor in Rome. Many people outside of Rome who had regionalist sympathies became Arians: they thereby identified themselves as culturally and regionally distinct from Rome. They used the Arian controversy to insist that, even if the political power of the emperor continued, at least the ecclesiastical power of the church in Rome was to be overthrown in favor of the local bishops' religious customs and the ecclesiastical government by regional bishops.

Constantine was aware that the Arian controversy was being used as a vehicle of protest against his power. He insisted that the church resolve the Arian controversy and thus eliminate the channel through which the regionalist bishops' protests against Roman rule were being funneled.

The First Council of Nicaea in 325 C.E.

The Council at Nicaea responded both to Constantine's demand for unity and to Arius's denial that Jesus was God by insisting that Jesus and the God are of the same substance. The bishops at Nicaea defined that Jesus was *homoousios,* that is, "of the same substance," as God. The Council formulated its doctrine about the identity of Jesus in the form of a universal creed that not only asserted the doctrine of the church, but also condemned Arian belief. Next the Council insisted that all of the bishops in attendance were to swear to the new Nicene creed. Then all members of the church community were to profess the anti-Arian creed that had been drawn up at Nicaea.

Nicene Creed

We believe in one God, the Father almighty, creator of all things both visible and invisible. And in our Lord Jesus Christ, the Son of God, the only begotten born of the Father, that is, of the substance of the Father; God from God, light from light, true God from true God; begotten, not created, consubstantial with the Father; through him all things were made, those in heaven and those on earth as well. For the sake of us men and for our salvation, he came down, was made flesh, and became man; he suffered and on the third day arose; he ascended into heaven and is going to come to judge the living and the dead. And we believe in the Holy Spirit.

As for those who say: "There was a time when he did not exist"; and, "Before he was begotten he did not exist"; and "He was made from nothing, or from another hypostasis or essence," alleging that the Son of God is mutable or subject to change—such persons the Catholic and apostolic Church condemns.[7]

The Responses of the Bishops to the Council of Nicaea

Many bishops participated in the Council. According to one record the total number of bishops at Nicaea was 318, though according to another there may have been as few as 200.

Most of the bishops agreed to swear to the Nicene Creed. However two of those bishops were so committed to their own regional authority that they refused. They deeply resented the centralized church's claim of authority over the expression of belief by all members. Consequently they refused to swear to the creed and accepted deposition from their sees and banishment from the empire. In response other regionalist bishops, who had already signed the new creed, changed their position and recanted their allegiance to the Nicene Creed and to the authority of the centralized church.

They knew that they too would be deposed and banished. Indeed Constantine intervened by threatening to exile any who did not swear to the creed. He ordered the bishops who had changed their position to be replaced in their churches and exiled from the empire.

Evidently their refusal to swear to the new creed was their expression both of regional autonomy and of opposition to the continuing power of the centralized church at Rome. The Arian protest again resumed its widespread appeal to much of the Mediterranean and European world. Nicaea's condemnation of Arius had not crushed the growing regionalism of the non-Roman cultures within the empires.

The Effect of Nicaea on Arianism

The Arians appeared again to be growing after the Council of Nicaea. The anti-Arian bishops were surrounded by a growing number of bishops who were either Arian or at least regionalists. In fact the majority of bishops within the empire, East and West, seemed to be Arian. Perhaps they were in fact more committed to their regional autonomy than to the actual theological doctrine of the Arians. However they expressed that insistence by demanding that the Arian doctrine be tolerated in those who chose so to believe.

The church at Rome responded to the renewed crisis by applying the Rule of Faith to the doctrine of Arius: the church fully intended to express in its doctrine on Jesus Christ the belief of the faithful communities in the church. However the application of the Rule of Faith to the Arian controversy became complex at that point.

The complexity was the result of the shadow that the desire for regional autonomy by so many bishops had cast over the belief of the faith communities. On the level of vocal and empirically verified expression, many bishops of the communities confessed the Arian belief: Jesus Christ, even if he might be the Savior, could not be God. However on the level of the silent, but genuine belief of the general population, the communities confessed complete reliance upon the divine Jesus Christ. What they were no longer willing to accept, because their bishops had led them to think autonomously, was the centralized authority that came from the political or ecclesiastical centers of the Roman Empire. Thus the church at Rome had difficulty formulating doctrine that the communities could identify as their own belief.

Response to Renewal of Arianism—the Rule of Faith

A pollster might conclude that the Roman church should have modified its doctrine and taught the doctrine of the Arians. The majority of the decision makers, the bishops in the Mediterranean and European cultures, appeared to explicitly confess the Arian faith. A claim that the faithful believers privately agreed with the Nicene Creed appeared to be no more than a hypothesis.

On the other hand a social psychologist might conclude that the bishops' explicit, vocal expression of belief had little or nothing to do with the private belief of the communities at a distance from Rome.

However, the church had access neither to pollsters nor social psychologists. Yet it still needed to discern the Spirit amidst the turbulence of the renewed Arian protest within the communities of believers.

Moreover the church needed to discern the faith of the community as it was expressed in the long-standing, tensive theological dialectic between the church at Antioch and the church at Alexandria. Both Antioch and Alexandria confessed that there were in Christ Jesus both a human and a divine nature. However the community at Antioch insisted that the one individual, Christ Jesus, was a human who also had a divine nature. The community at Alexandria on the other hand insisted that the one individual, Christ Jesus, was the divine one who also had a human nature.

As a result, the church centered at Rome found itself caught in the tension caused by two distinct quandaries—that of Arianism and that of the Antioch-Alexandria dialectic. It needed to resolve both by the Rule of Faith. The task of discerning the belief of the Christian community was complex. The church authorities needed a standard by which to discern the belief of the community.

The hymns used by the faith communities in worship ought to provide such a standard. Yet those hymns might just as well express the regionalist yearning of the communities as well as their belief. Nonetheless the church needed to commit itself to discerning what belief the Spirit had revealed in the expressions of faith used by the communities gathered in worship of Jesus Christ.

Thus, the church confronted its task and set itself to discern the belief that it hoped would lead to defining a doctrinal identity that was revealed in the expressions of the communities' belief.

VI. The Development of the Controversies Leading Up to Chalcedon: The Dialectic between Antioch and Alexandria

The discussion of hymns that had been used in the era just prior to the Council of Chalcedon had anticipated the momentous turn in Christology that the Council of Chalcedon would mark in 451 C.E.

We must now back up to a perspective that permits us to observe the historical developments that led up to the convening of the Council at Chalcedon, which would fix a theological definition in response to the Christological dialectic that caught the empires in its swirl of conflict.

The dialectic that determined the tensions over belief in Christ was mirrored in the dialectic between the beliefs of the fourth-and fifth-century communities at Antioch and Alexandria. That dialectic had been exacerbated by the Arian controversy.

Arianism in the Controversy between
Antioch and Alexandria

The community at Antioch believed that Christ was the only human who ever had two natures. A growing number of Arians, in harmony with Antioch's insistence that Christ was partially human and not entirely divine, believed that the one individual who was Christ was not simply God.

The Arians insisted upon approaching Christ "from below," from the perspective that he was not the God. As they argued, "Once God was alone, and not yet a Father, but afterwards he became a Father." The Son had a beginning—he was "begotten by the Father." It followed in Arian thinking that before the Son's beginning the Father had not yet fathered the Begotten One and thus was not the "Father" God. They argued, since God had "created" wisdom (Prv 8:22-31) "before the age," hence God had created both *Logos* and the Son of God. Therefore the *Logos* was for the Arians a cosmological intermediary between the status of humans and the status of God. Yet the *Logos* was not one who was by nature a divine being. He may have remained a good, perhaps even a perfect human being by his own free will, but not by virtue of oneness of essence with God. Christ's human moral progress had won for him the title Son of God. Thus for the Arians Christ was on the one hand a non-divine being who had been created by God before the ages. On the other hand Christ was enriched with the title Son of God because of his perfection as a human individual. Thus the Arians placed Christ on a level higher than the human level, but lower than the divine.[1]

Furthermore the Arians used Mark 13:32 ("But of that day or that hour no one knows, not indeed the angels, nor the Son, but only the Father") to argue that the Son was ignorant of the hour of the last judgment: he lacked the omniscience that he would have if he were God.[2]

The Antiochenes assumed that humans can speak about Christ only in terms which they would use to speak about anyone. Their perspective was that humans can make judgments about human existence, but cannot make a judgment about the characteristics of the existence of God. Thus Christ might be the most sublime of humans, the unique savior of all humans, the redeemer, even the adopted Son of God. He might even deserve to be known as God. However humans cannot speak about Christ as God in a manner that suggests that they know anything about the divine existence. The Antiochenes understood Christ to have been created from nothing by the Father in order to be the instrument for creating the world. Therefore he was the uniquely sublime Wisdom by which God created everything; yet, the Wisdom that God used in creating could not have been the same as the God who used that Wisdom.

On the other hand, the church at Alexandria approached Christ "from above," or from the perspective that permits us to assert about Christ what we can assert only about God. Alexandrian theology held that humans were able to make judgments about the characteristics of the existence of God. Thus even though Christ might have been born of Mary and therefore shared in being human, nonetheless Mary had conceived Jesus by the overshadowing of the Holy Spirit. She is the mother of God. Christ must therefore be understood to be fundamentally the divine one, not simply a human.

The dialectic between those two positions had been carried on at least from the third century, but more acutely during the fourth and fifth centuries. That dialectical tension was significant enough to draw the focus away from the Arian controversy. The Antiochene-Alexandrian dialectic contributed a tone to the definition of Christ distinct from that contributed by the Arian controversy.

On the one hand the dialectic between the theologies of

Antioch and Alexandria challenged the belief of all who were in the church, and challenges all who are now in the church, to focus upon the dialectical tension that Christians have always recognized in their belief in Christ: namely, the tension between reason, which asserts that Christ was human, and imaginative belief, which asserts that Christ existed in such a unique relationship with God that among humans he consciously acted in the place of God.

On the other hand the cultural and communal unrest caused by the Arian controversy confronted the church with the need to resolve the dialectic concerning the identity of Christ, to settle upon a universally accepted category of his identity.

When the church did select a method of resolving the dialectic, she used one that embraced neither a sociopolitical resolution (favored by the emperor), nor a rational, theological argument about creeds (used by the Arians), but a respect for the communal belief expressed by the church's communities. The chosen criterion was the Rule of Faith, which would provide the church with the method of articulating that identity of Jesus Christ which the Holy Spirit, moving within the faith of those communities, had been leading the church to discover.

The Continued Growth of Arianism after Its Condemnation

The Antioch-Alexandria dialectic had been subsumed into the Arian controversy because of the widespread acceptance of the Arian definition of Christ as not divine. Because the Antiochians had also stressed the human identity of Christ, the Antiochene position came to be identified with the Arian position.

There were a great number of bishops who had defected

from the doctrine held by the Roman church to that of the Arian position. Many of those bishops had previously sworn to confess the creed of the Council at Nicaea, but later defected either because of a shift in their beliefs or because of regionalism. As a result of the swelling of the number of those who espoused the Arian position, the Arian controversy resumed its former power in the fifth century; again the Arian debates generated civil unrest within the Roman Empire.

Because there were so many supporters of the Arian position, even after its condemnation by the Council of Nicaea, there was strong support among the Arians to remain fixed in their defiance and to refuse to switch from the Arian confession to that of the church in Rome.

The evidence that the Arians fomented just such an ecclesiastical rebellion is found in the letters that Arius wrote to his supporters. In those letters to influential churchmen Arius urged his followers to revolt, rather than to obey.

Letter by Arius to Eusebius of Nicomedia
(c. 335 C.E.)
(Eusebius, bishop of Nicomedia, was the leader of those who supported the Arian belief in the first half of the fourth century. He and Arius had earlier been disciples of Lucian at Antioch. After Arius's deposition by Alexander, the Patriarch of Alexandria, Eusebius continued openly to espouse the Arian cause. Eusebius thereby transformed the Arian controversy from being a dispute between an Egyptian patriarch and his unorthodox preacher to being an ecumenical controversy that was to spread throughout the empires of Rome and Constantinople.)

To his most dear Lord, Eusebius, a man of God, faithful and orthodox, Arius, the man unjustly persecuted by the Pope Alexander for the all-conquering truth's sake, of which thou too art a champion, sends health in the Lord. As Ammonius, my father, was going to Nicomedia, it seemed becoming to address this through him; and withal to represent to that deep-seated affection which thou bearest towards the brethren for the sake of God and His Christ, how fiercely the bishop assaults and drives us, leaving no means untried in his opposition. At length he has driven us out of the city, as men without God, for dissenting from his public declarations, that, "As God is eternal, so is His Son: where the Father, there the Son; the Son coexists in God without a beginning [or birth]: ever generate, an ingenerately-generate; that neither in idea, nor by an instant of time, does God precede the Son; an eternal God, an eternal Son; the Son is from God Himself." Since then, Eusebius, thy brother of Caesarea, Theodotus, Paulinus, & c... and all the bishops of the East declare that God exists without origin before the Son, they are made anathema by Alexander's sentence; all but Philogonius, Hellanicus, and Macarius, heretical, ill-grounded men, who say, one that He is an utterance, another an offspring, another coingenerate. These blasphemies we cannot bear even to hear; no, not if the heretics should threaten us with ten thousand deaths. What, on the other hand, are our statements and opinions, our past and present teaching? That the Son is not ingenerate, nor in any way a part of the Ingenerate, nor made of any subject-matter; but that, by the will and counsel of God, He subsisted before times and ages, perfect God, Only-begotten, unchangeable; and that before this generation, or creation, or determination, or establishment, He was not, for He is not ingenerate. And we are persecuted for saying, the Son has an origin, but God is unoriginate; for this we are under persecution, and for saying that He is out of nothing, inasmuch as He is neither part of God, nor of any subject-matter. Therefore we are persecuted; the rest thou knowest. I pray that thou be strong in the Lord, remembering our afflictions, fellow-Lucianist, truly named Eusebius.[3]

Arius was addressing the words of the creed that had been drawn up by the Council of Nicaea; namely:

We believe in one God the Father Almighty, Maker of all
things visible and invisible; and in one Lord Jesus Christ,
the Son of God, begotten of the Father, only-begotten,
that is, from the substance of the Father, God from God,
Light from Light, True God from True God, begotten not
made, of one substance with the Father, through whom
all things were made.[4]

The position of Arius the polemicist in this letter is
quite different from the position of Arius the hymn writer,
presented in the third chapter. Yet in both cases Arius was
careful to insist upon the humanity and the divinity of
Christ Jesus, while he was also careful not to claim to be
able to categorize precisely the relationship between Christ
Jesus and the God. On the other hand he had presumed
that he was able to assert precisely the extent to which
humans can distinguish between the Christ, who was
begotten by God, and God.

Alexandria's Position in the Dialectic

A second letter by Arius reveals the tension that he
acknowledged between the position of the church at Antioch
that seemed to support his belief and the greater-than-human
position held by the church at Alexandria. The letter provides
evidence of the extent to which Arius went in claiming to be
capable of grasping the relationship between Christ and God:
he recognized in that relationship no mystery for his human
comprehension.

Letter of Arius to Alexander
*(Alexander was the bishop of Alexandria beginning in 313 C.E.
and during the Arian controversy. He was actively concerned in
putting down the Arian schism. At a council of his clergy at
Alexandria [c. 321 C.E.] he excommunicated Arius.)*

To Alexander, our blessed Primate and Bishop, the Priests and Deacons send health in the Lord. Our hereditary faith, which thou too, blessed Primate, has taught us, is this: We believe in One God, alone ingenerate, alone everlasting, alone unoriginate, alone truly God, alone immortal, alone wise, alone good, alone sovereign, alone judge of all, ordainer and dispenser, unchangeable and unalterable, just and good, of the Law and the Prophets, and of the New Covenant. We believe that this God gave birth to the Only-begotten Son before age-long times, through whom He has made those ages themselves, and all things else; that He generated Him, not in semblance, but in truth, giving Him a real subsistence [or *hypostasis*], at His own will, so as to be unchangeable and unalterable, God's perfect creature, but not as other creatures, His production, but not as other productions; nor as Valentinus maintained, an offspring [*probole*]; nor again, as Manichaeus, a consubstantial part; nor, as Sabellius, a Son-Father, which is to make two out of one; nor, as Hieracas, one torch from another, or a flame divided into two; nor, as if He were previously in being, and afterwards generated or created again to be a Son, a notion condemned by thyself, blessed Primate, in full Church and among the assembled Clergy; but, as we affirm, created at the will of God before times and before ages, and having life and being from the Father, who gave subsistence as to Him, so to His glorious perfections. For, when the Father gave to Him the inheritance of all things, He did not thereby deprive Himself of attributes, which are His ingenerately, who is the Source of all things.

So there are Three Subsistences [or Persons]; and whereas God is the Cause of all things, and therefore unoriginate simply by Himself, the Son on the other hand, born of the Father time-apart, and created and established before all periods, did not exist before He was born, but being born of the Father time-apart, was brought into substantive existence [subsistence], He alone by the Father alone. For He is not eternal, or coeternal, or coingenerate with the Father; nor hath an existence together with the Father, as if there were two ingenerate Origins; but God is before all things, as being a Monad, and the Origin of all; — and therefore before the Son also, as indeed we have learned from thee in thy public preaching. Inasmuch then as it is from God that He hath His being, and His glorious perfections, and His life, and His charge of all things, for this reason God is His Origin, as being His God and before Him. As to such phrases as "from Him," and "from the womb," and "issued forth from the Father, and am come," if they be understood, as they are by some, to denote a part of the consubstantial, and a *probole* [offspring], then the Father will be of a compound nature, and divisible, and changeable, and corporeal; and thus, as far as their words go, the incorporeal God will be subjected to the properties of matter. I pray for thy health in the Lord, blessed Primate.[5]

This letter of Arius reveals that he had reduced the relationship of Christ Jesus and the Father to such a logical relationship that he could grasp it in terms of the categories of human analysis that were appropriate for understanding any human experience. Such logical categories are indeed adequate for rational analysis of human experiences, but less than adequate for the comprehension of the relationship between Christ Jesus and God, which is a mystery.

Christology Centered upon "the Mother of God"

The individual who was Christ Jesus was a creature for Arius and the Arians; he might have been for them the most sublime human person, even the only begotten Son of God, but not God. Therefore Mary, the mother of Jesus, could not have been the mother of God. She could have been no more than the mother of Jesus, the mother of a creature.

The Arian refusal to acknowledge that Mary was the mother of God challenged the doctrine of the church centered at Alexandria in Egypt. The Alexandrian church had long identified Mary as the mother of God. That identity was derived from the Alexandrian church's insistence that Jesus of Nazareth must be identified as divine.

Therefore because Jesus was a divine being, Mary, the mother of Jesus, must have been the mother of a divine being. She was the mother of God. The Holy Spirit generated Jesus.

At the contrary pole the theologians at Antioch proclaimed Mary the mother of the human Jesus. Antiochene theology developed a "Christology from below," which presumed to speak about Christ only from within the contours of space and time.

Thus the Christological controversy had drawn its line of battle at the point of the identification of Mary: either she was the mother of the human Jesus because Jesus was human, or she was the mother of God because Jesus was divine.

Political Involvement in the Christological Controversy

The church at Alexandria was fortunate enough to win over Marcian, the husband and consort of Pulcheria, the regent empress of the Eastern Roman Empire.

Pulcheria was the daughter of the Emperor Arcadius and his wife Eudoxia. During the reign of the emperor Arcadius, Eudoxia had controlled her weak husband to the extent that she functioned as empress.

Then Pulcheria and her brother, Theodosius II, had become coempress and coemperor in 404 C.E. at the death of Eudoxia. Imitating her mother, Pulcheria manipulated her weak brother, so that she was able to reign independently, instead of sharing the position with her brother. As empress she was expected to have a consort, but out of piety she had taken a private vow of virginity. Thus she needed a consort who would not be interested in marital relations. One suspects that she also wanted a consort who would permit her to function as empress. Her choice fell upon a pious, sixty-year-old, retired soldier, Marcian.

By 450 C.E. he had taken over the function of overseeing religion in the Eastern Empire. He had long endorsed Alexandrian Christology and thus uncompromisingly had insisted that Jesus of Nazareth was to be understood as thoroughly divine.

As Constantine had summoned the Council of Nicaea to resolve the tension in the empire that had been caused by the first stage of the Arian controversy, so Marcian summoned a council to resolve the tension caused by the rebirth of the Arian controversy and the bitter conflict between Antioch and Alexandria about the mother of God.

The council was to be held at Chalcedon, directly across the Straits of the Bosporus from the capital of the Eastern Empire, Constantinople. Marcian was confident that he would be able to manipulate the decision of the assembled bishops so that they would espouse his definition of Christ, the definition formulated by the church at Alexandria.

The bishops assembled at Chalcedon in the autumn of 451 C.E. under the shadow of control that was cast upon them by the Emperor Marcian. However another shadow then loomed: the authority of the Pope, Leo the Great.

Influence of Pope Leo's *Tome*

Pope Leo the Great had significantly advanced and consolidated the central authority of the Roman papacy. He pressed his claim to have jurisdiction over the church throughout Europe and Africa.

In 449 C.E. Pope Leo issued his "*Tome*" in order to impose his authority upon the Council's bishops. Leo ordered them to endorse a Christology that would make it evident that Christ had redeemed all human individuals.

Pope Leo based his claim to centralized authority and his demand for obedience by the bishops upon an ancient tradition in the church: the Word of God, the theological term for Jesus Christ in his relation with the Father, was present in the church through the office that the pope and the bishops exercised in their ecclesiastical offices and liturgies. The traditional understanding in the Latin church was that Christ, the Word of God, the *Logos,* gave instruction to the church through the pope and the bishops and thereby conferred upon the baptized the power to believe and obey that instruction.[6] The *Logos,* who had appeared in Jesus Christ, is thus the principle not only of creation, but also of the faith that grounds the authority of the Roman church.

The *Tome* of Leo argued that the Council bishops needed to define the identity of Christ so that the *Logos* functioned actively within the papal office which proclaimed the universal salvation won by Christ Jesus.

In the *Logos* and in a variety of such metaphors, Pope Leo and the bishops who shared his understanding of salvation expressed their conviction that salvation had been accomplished by a being who was in no way inferior to the Lord of heaven and earth. The Redeemer did not therefore belong to some lower or intermediate order of reality, but was God.

The *Logos* in the Rule of Faith

However Pope Leo's doctrinal conviction does not appear to align with the doctrine of the Rule of Faith as that had developed in previous centuries; Leo apparently intended to identify his authoritarian conviction as imposed doctrine.

Nevertheless there had been a dialogue within the church regarding Jesus Christ as the Son of God and the *Logos*.

The *Second Letter of Clement* (c. 97 C.E.), the oldest surviving sermon of the Christian church apart from the New Testament's sermons, opened with the words:

> Brethren, we ought so to think of Jesus Christ as God, as of the judge of the living and dead. For him, being the Son of God, we adore, but the martyrs we cherish (2 Clem 1:1-2).[7]

Theophilus of Antioch had argued in the late second century in his letter to Autolycus: "God had this *Logos* as a helper in the things that were created by him; by him God made all things."[8]

Also in the third century Tertullian (c. 160-225 C.E.) in his *De carne Christi* praised the salvation accomplished by Christ as the work of God, "not of an intercessor, nor of an angel, but of the Lord himself. For Tertullian Christ as Lord was identifiable as the Yahweh of the Hebrews."[9]

These early writings make clear the belief of the ancient church: the one who had come in Christ and who continued to reign from the cross was no less than the supreme God himself.

Later, Theodore of Mopsuestia (350-428 C.E.), a leading Antiochene theologian, insisted in his *Catechetical Homilies* that the *Logos* was impassable, a doctrine which the church in Alexandria had also taught. The *Logos* could not be destroyed, even if his body was executed on the cross.

Further, Cyril of Alexandria (d. 444 C.E.) had insisted that the words of Psalm 94:22, which prayed to the God who had "become" humanity's refuge, did not mean that God had ceased being God, nor that God had become something that he had not been from the beginning. God is unchangeable by nature and remains what he was and ever is, even though he is said to have "become" in Christ a refuge for humanity. Cyril argued that the psalm meant, when the *Logos* was being transformed into the nature of flesh, he was not changed in his divine immutability, but continued to be divine while he dwelt among humanity.[10]

Finally Nestorius of Antioch, who had lived immediately before the Council of Chalcedon, taught in his *Letter to Cyril* (cf. above) that Christ was indeed impassable, even according to the nature of his body.[11] Yet Nestorius also used the gospels (Lk 2:52)—"And Jesus increased"—to teach that Jesus had developed, as any human must. The human Jesus had grown not only in stature, but in wisdom and in grace. Thus Nestorius's interpretation of Jesus Christ's identity was dialectical or ambiguous.[12]

As a result of this development, one would expect that the bishops at Chalcedon would have responded to the influence of the emperor, the pope, and the theological tradition, and readily endorsed Alexandria's Christology from above, that Christ was God. They would have been well aware of the mounting of theological data—from Tertullian, Theodore, Cyril, Nestorius, and Pope Leo, to define that the one who was Christ was none other than the divine One.

But the bishops at Chalcedon were also aware that a more nuanced tradition had been passed down to the communities. That tradition is represented in the writings of Nestorius, who proposed that Christ was to be grasped not only as divine, but also as human. In his *Sermons on the Theotokos* Nestorius expounded how the divine and the human in Christ coincided in their appearance and so were one: there was a genuine indwelling of the divine *Logos* in the man Jesus. In that sense there was a genuine incarnation of the *Logos*.[13] The tensive interrelation between the divine and the human in Christ was carefully preserved in this theological tradition of the incarnation of the *Logos* as human. It stood alongside the other two traditions that emphasized Christ as either primarily divine or as primarily human.

Dialectical Christologies of Two Natures and One Person

Yet even within that tradition of the two natures in Christ there were conflicting Christologies regarding the manner in which Christ was both divine and human.

There was the Christology of the hypostatic union, which Athanasius of Alexandria (c. 296-373 C.E.) taught, for example in his *Orations against the Arians*. That interpretation of Christ took as its point of departure the Gospel according to John ("And the Word became flesh...." Jn 1:14); there was an indivisible unity between the *Logos* and flesh. Athanasius had insisted that the Son of God had become the Son of Man.

There was also the Christology of the indwelling *Logos,* which Apollinarius (c. 310-90 C.E.) had taught. That interpretation of Christology insisted that the divine and the human in Christ were not equal components. On the contrary the one individual who was Christ Jesus may have exercised a human nature, but acted in virtue of the divine nature: the nature of the one who was Christ was the nature of the *Logos*.[14]

As a result before Chalcedon there had been in the Christian tradition a tensive theology, a dialectic concerning the two natures in Christ: one theology keeping the two natures on a par, the other subordinating one nature to the other.

The Syrians—Theodore of Mopsuestia, Barsumas of Nisibis, and Babai the Great—explicitly articulated that tensive Christology: they refused to polarize its interpretation of the one who was Christ as being the same as either of the two natures. They held that Christ was not the same as the nature of the divine one nor the same as the nature of the human one. Rather when the Syrians referred to the divine and the human in Christ, they used the language for two natures. Yet when that theology referred to the concrete person of Jesus Christ, even when it referred to Christ as the incarnate *Logos*, it then chose to refer not to a nature, but to one person.

That position of the Syrians is expressed even by Cyril of Alexandria in his exposition of the verse from the Gospel of Luke, "In those days he went out to the mountain to pray; and all night he continued in prayer to God" (Lk 6:12). Cyril devoutly respected the gospels as the Word of God. Yet he was also open to the more subtle implications of that Word. The passage from Luke portrayed Jesus Christ as a human being who sought God in prayer. Jesus was for Luke not a person who experienced an immediate intimacy with God.[15]

Moreover Cyril, in his *On the Incarnation of the Only Begotten*, confessed: "For my part I say that it is appropriate neither for the *Logos* of God apart from the humanity, nor for the temple born of the woman not united to the *Logos* to be called Christ Jesus." When Cyril wrote about Christ as the object of Christian devotion and as the bringer of salvation, he did use the pattern of concentrating not upon the one who possessed the union of the two natures, but upon the one who was incarnate. He generally referred to the one incarnate *Logos,* truly and fully both God and man, as the Savior.[16]

Of greatest significance to the fathers who gathered at Chalcedon, however, was Leo's *Tome,* which also proposed a tensive Christology. The *Tome* reflected upon Philippians 2:7, "but he emptied himself," to teach that the bending down of the *Logos* had been an action of compassion, not a surrender of power. Thus the two natures were for Leo distinctly preserved in the one person. The passible humanity was joined to the impassible divinity. Leo found further evidence of such a tensive Christology in the gospels, which envisioned not only Christ in the swaddling clothes and on the cross, but also Christ before whom the Magi adored and Christ by whose words the gates of heaven opened to the thief on the cross.

Consequently Leo insisted that the fathers at Chalcedon avoid an extreme Christology based on a hypostatic union; namely, that the one who was Jesus was unequivocally the *Logos*.[17]

Definition of the Identity of Christ Jesus by Chalcedon

In an act of surprising autonomy, the bishops endorsed neither the position of Alexandria, Antioch, Arius, nor Leo. Rather they formulated a position that represented a synthesis of all those positions.

They drew upon a variety of theological sources as precedents for their definition of the identity of Christ Jesus. Among those sources were (a) the *Second Letter of Cyril to Nestorius*—from perhaps 430 C.E.; (b) the *Tome* of Leo, especially Leo's insistence that in any definition of a hypostatic union, the differences of Christ's natures remain unconfused; (c) Theodoret (393-466 C.E.), bishop of Cyrus in Syria, who insisted that there was a duality in Christ that could be expressed with the phrase, used by Chalcedon, "neither divided nor separated into two persons."[18]

The bishops adopted from these sources a theology that formulated the identity of Christ Jesus as an integration of the pluralism of beliefs expressed in the theologies of the various writings.

The definition of the bishops at the Council of Chalcedon first reaffirmed the definition of Christ by the Councils of Nicaea and Constantinople: namely, Jesus Christ is "of the same substance" as God the Father. Then it insisted that Mary is "the Mother of God"; in other words, the humanity of Christ is separable from his divinity: there is no confusion of the two natures in Christ. Rather there are two discrete natures in one hypostasis. Jesus Christ is fully human and fully divine; moreover the believer must affirm both natures in a dialectic, viewing neither one nor the other as separable.

The Council established a synthetic, Christological model that all believers were to follow: namely, the identity of Christ as both fully human and fully divine.

Moreover the bishops insisted that nothing could be said about Jesus as divine that would deny his humanity; nor could anything be said about his humanity that would deny his divinity; there was "no interchange of characters." Thus, after the definition at Chalcedon the believer was to affirm not only that Christ Jesus is human—his humanity is not altered by his divinity—but also that Christ Jesus is divine—that his divinity is not altered by his humanity. Thus the believer needs always to affirm that Christ Jesus is both human and divine, neither only human nor only divine.

However the formula of definition of Christ by Chalcedon, while insisting on two natures without separation in the one hypostasis who is Christ, ignored the problems that ignited the Christological controversy. That is, the definition of Chalcedon failed to explain how the subject, Jesus Christ, could learn as a boy, grow to manhood, suffer, die, and yet be "of the same substance" as God.

The fathers at Chalcedon defended their definition by claiming that they had repeated the theology of the fathers at Nicaea. However all participants in the Christological controversy made that claim. Though the Council's claim to have repeated Nicaea should have been defended by a detailed analysis of the relationship between Nicaea and Chalcedon, there was no such analysis.[19]

As a result, the Council's decisions confronted the church at large and most especially the Alexandrians with an apparent endorsement of the Antiochian position. Furthermore the fathers at Chalcedon were conscious that if they uncritically endorsed Alexandria's "Christology from above" and asserted that Christ Jesus was divine without reference to his being human, then they would have rejected the belief of those communities who confessed him to be their human brother and Lord.

Consequently those believers who endorsed the Alexandrian Christology were challenged to modify their position and to confess that there was value in the Antiochian position: namely, that Jesus was indeed fully human. The Alexandrian believers were nonetheless permitted, but with a tensive dialectic, to endorse their own position: Jesus is fully divine.

However the Alexandrian believers judged that the church at Chalcedon had given far too much ground to Antioch, far too little to Alexandria.

The Alexandrian faith had been heavily influenced by the Platonic tradition of the reality of the spiritual world. Cyril of Alexandria wrote of such a spiritual view of the identity of Christ Jesus in his *Second Letter to Nestorius of Antioch*:

> We do not say that the *Logos* became flesh by having his nature changed, nor for that matter that he was transformed into a complete human being composed out of soul and body. On the contrary, we say that in an unspeakable and incomprehensible way, the *Logos* united to himself, in his hypostasis, flesh enlivened by a rational soul, and in this way became a human being and has been designated "Son of man." He did not become a human being simply by an act of will or "good pleasure," any more than he did so by merely taking on a person.

> "...the idea is not that he found the beginning of his existence inside the holy Virgin, nor is it that he necessarily stood in need of a second birth through her in addition to his birth from the Father, for it is at once stupid and pointless to assert that one who exists prior to every age, coeternal with the Father, is in need of a second birth through her in addition to his birth from the Father, for it is at once stupid and pointless to assert that one who exists prior to every age, coeternal with the Father, is in

need of a second way of coming into being. Since, however , the *Logos* was born of a woman after he had, "for us
and for our salvation," united human reality hypostati-
cally to himself, he is said on this ground to have had a
fleshly birth. It is not the case that first of all an ordinary
human being was born of the holy Virgin and that the
Logos descended upon him subsequently. On the contrary, since the union took place in the very womb, he is
said to have undergone a fleshly birth by making his
own the birth of the flesh which belonged to him.[20]

On the other hand the Antiochene faith had been influenced by the Aristotelian tradition of reality as fashioned by
complementary components. Its theology of Christ Jesus
insisted that the one who was Christ exercised the comple-
ments of both the divine and human natures. To express this,
Antiochene theology had used linguistic ambiguities.

For example Nestorius of Antioch wrote to Cyril of
Alexandria an explanation of the Antiochene faith in the loose
union of divine and human natures in Christ Jesus:

> Observe how [the fathers of Nicaea] first of all establish,
> as foundations, the titles, which are common to deity
> and the humanity—"Lord" and "Jesus" and "Christ" and
> "Only Begotten" and "Son"—and then build on them the
> teaching about his becoming human and his passion
> and resurrection, in order that, since the titles which sig-
> nify and are common to both natures are set in the fore-
> ground, the things which pertain to the sonship and
> lordship are not divided and the things peculiar to the
> natures within the unitary sonship do not get endan-
> gered by the suggestion of a confusion.[21]

The intention of Nestorius appears to have been to hide
the complementaries of the one who was Christ Jesus within
the linguistic ambiguities of that text.

The fathers at the Council of Chalcedon had chosen

neither the clarity of Alexandria's spiritual worldview of Christ as divine, nor the linguistic ambiguities of Antioch's loose unity of two complementaries in Christ. Rather they fashioned their definition of Christ's identity in a manner that not only bridged the worldviews of those two churches (note the tension between the "fully human" and the "fully divine" in their definition), but also expressed the tensive faith of the believing communities. The definition of Chalcedon acknowledged that Christ Jesus is both fully human and fully divine. Yet the Council also insisted that one cannot confess him to have been only one. One must confess him to be both human and divine, but not only human nor only divine.

Prior to the Council of Chalcedon and foreshadowing the definition of the Council, both Hilary of Poitiers (315-67 C.E.) and Theodore of Mopsuestia (c. 350-428 C.E.) had taught that the New Testament was ambiguous about Christ's nature.

Theodore had argued that, on the one hand, the New Testament presented Christ as a human who was expected to satisfy the demands of the law for humans and who addressed God as other humans address God. On the other hand, as Theodore argued, it also presented Christ as divine in himself: he suffered for our salvation.[22]

Hilary, the leading and most respected Latin theologian of his age and an anti-Arian, argued that Christ had been divine before the incarnation (*ante hominem Deus*), was both divine and human during his *kenosis,* his human life on earth (*homo et Deus*), and is completely human and completely God in his exaltation.[23]

Thus the bishops at Chalcedon had theological precedents for their definition that the identification of Christ needed to be asserted tensively.

The Doctrine of Chalcedon and the Rule of Faith

One can only ask what motivation led the Council of Chalcedon to formulate such a definition, especially since the pressures under which the bishops at Chalcedon worked must have tilted them toward Alexandria's Christology from above, toward endorsing the identity of Christ as God.

However when they finally hammered out their definition, they did not endorse that position. Rather they defined Jesus Christ as one who can be identified only by a tensive dialectic between a human nature and a divine nature. What had influenced the assembled bishops so to reformulate the theology of Christ Jesus?

The study of the early hymns again suggests an answer to that question. They reveal that the community of believers had apparently from the very beginning of Christianity expressed their belief in the identity of Christ tensively. Their Lord had always been understood by them as both human and divine.

That dialectical faith has been presented previously. The third chapter of this study of the early Christian hymns suggests that the fathers at Chalcedon had presented the bipolar belief of the Christian communities. The early hymns, as well as the doctrine of Chalcedon, confess that Christ Jesus is both human and divine. He is the one only in relation to the other. Such was the faith expressed in the early hymns. Such, as well, was the doctrine expressed at Chalcedon.

The Rule of Faith at this point provides a cardinal perspective upon the work of Chalcedon. According to the Rule of Faith the church must be careful to express as doctrine that which the community has been expressing as its belief. Thus the bishops at Chalcedon were challenged to formulate as doctrine neither the doctrine of Emperor Marcian, nor of Alexandria, nor of Antioch, nor of Arius, and not even that of Pope Leo, but the belief of the regional communities. That faith may indeed have been mirrored partially—but only partially—by various expressions of anyone of those communities.

The Council also went beyond the doctrines discerned by the Rule of Faith. It added the carefully worded refinement that neither identity of Christ—human nor divine—was to modify the other position. Thus the Chalcedonian doctrine insisted that in confessing Christ to be divine, one must not alter anything in his human nature that would make him other than human. So too it insisted that in confessing him to be human, one must not alter anything in his divine nature that would make him other than divine.

At first this careful refinement that there must be no "exchange of characteristics" might appear to be little more than a shadow cast by a metaphysical cloud. However the contrary is the case. It should be clear that this condition significantly restricts any befogging of Christ's humanity when speaking of a Christology from above. Thus, the fully human Christ Jesus must have felt with human emotions, must have known with human understanding, must have had human awareness of God, must have willed humanly, must have resisted temptation with a human capacity, and so on.

A theology from below is far less restricted by the condition of no exchange of characteristics: it cannot discuss Jesus' humanity so that he would be other than the God. However since humans have almost no knowledge about the identity of God, almost nothing can be said about Jesus Christ as God.

For example, though many assert that God is almighty, that notion is an assumption worked out by biblical authors and by Aristotle. The biblical authors perhaps made that assertion in order to explain how God had exercised control of history; Aristotle, to complete his system of a hierarchy of metaphysical forms.

So too the notion that God cannot change was worked out by Plato because of his doctrine of the radiation of all from the One.

In short, the notions that humans assert about God have been worked out by human minds.

The issue relevant for the doctrine of the fathers at Chalcedon is that they insisted more upon the human identity of Christ Jesus than upon his divine identity, though they had nonetheless said that he had a divine nature. Yet even in so identifying him, they said very little that can be understood to elevate Christ Jesus out of his position on the plane of the human family.

The reader needs at this point to return to the Arian theology of Christ Jesus: the definition of Chalcedon came very close to endorsing that position. The refinement of the definition of Chalcedon by the "no exchange of characteristics" appears to have favored the Arians' insistence that Christ Jesus must be considered not as God, but as begotten by God. Christ Jesus can be considered as God only insofar as the divine nature is in relation to his human nature. The Arians held that only God can be considered to be divine unconditionally.

However, the Council bishops did not endorse the Arian position. The bishops at Chalcedon challenged believers to recognize and to assent to the subtle differences between the Arians' categorical definition of Christ as less than divine and Chalcedon's dialectical definition of Christ as more than human.

VII. The Need for Tensive Dialectic to Express Mystery

This study has thus far explored the tension that exists identification between some hymns' identification of Christ Jesus as human and others', as divine Lord. The early communities of believers preserved hymns that confessed both identities of their Lord. That tension, which reflects the belief of the fourth-and fifth-century communities of the church, challenges twentieth-century Western communities of belief.

Tensive Belief for Twentieth-Century Westerners

The less subtle, more empirical, twentieth-century communities of American believers might tend to select only hymns that confess one identity. There is in modern, Western communities the pragmatic value of reducing ambiguity to clarity. Contemporary Americans assume that, even if an occurrence appears to elude rational analysis, it needs to be presented in clear and distinct categories.

Thus, when the early hymns shift between alternate identities of Christ Jesus, they raise the suspicions of the American pragmatist: perhaps these early communities were unclear about how they identified Christ Jesus.

However upon further reflection on the tensive identification of Christ Jesus that those hymns express, one can conclude that the tension reflects the early communities' awareness that Jesus' identity is not clear and distinct, but rather a mystery. The choice of tensive language recognized that the mystery of Jesus' identity could be expressed only if the teachings about Jesus strained against one another. If his identity is genuinely enigmatic, perhaps they could only confess their belief in him by using language that expressed different identities. One kind of language pulls against the other.

Conversely the modern American pragmatist tends to reject a tensive description of an occurrence or a human individual. The pragmatist desires to remove the tensive language and substitute a language that situates the individual within the categories of human conventions.

Yet mystery does indeed confront individuals throughout life. Such mysteries defy neat classification into categories that render them comprehensible as clear and distinct. There is a tension between the apparent meaning of an occurrence and the elusive dynamism that operates in the same occurrence. The language appropriate to identify mysteries needs to be dual languages: one strains against the other. Consequently one cannot reduce mystery to concise categories.

Of course the critical thinker might here demand evidence that a tensive language is at times needed to discuss how certain experiences encounter humans. That evidence can be cited in the writings of at least two modern writers: Sir Ernest Shackleton and F. C. Happold. Though they had different encounters with mystery, they both had to tell their stories by using a language inherently inadequate to capture the full depth and scope of their experiences.

Sir Ernest Shackleton's Encounter with Mystery

Sir Ernest Shackleton encountered mystery during his extraordinary expedition to cross the South Pole on foot in 1914-16. As he and his team were trekking across Antarctica in order to return to their ship, they were caught in the midst of a severe winter storm. When they finally reached their ship, the *Endurance,* in January 1915, they discovered it had been crushed by an ice flow.

With no ship to carry them away from Antarctica, the team chose to establish a camp on a free expanse of ice. They drifted on the ice until April 1916, subsisting on seals and penguins. When the ice reached the Palmer Peninsula, they were still in Antarctica. Shackleton and two companions chose to set out in lifeboats on one of the most remarkable small-boat journeys in maritime history. In sixteen days they rowed nine hundred miles through a winter storm to South Georgia Island. The three exhausted men then had to march thirty-six hours across a glacier on South Georgia in order to reach a settlement where they could find people and help.

Shackleton later reflected upon that journey:

> I know that during that long and racking march of thirty-six hours over the unnamed mountains and glaciers of South Georgia it seemed to me often that we were four, not three. I said nothing to my companions on the point, but afterwards Worsley [one of other two] said to me, "Boss, I had a curious feeling on the march that there was another person with us." Crean [the other of the two] confessed to the same idea.

Shackleton later attempted to identify the meaning of the impression of the fourth member:

> When I look back at those days I have no doubt that Providence guided us, not only across those snowfields, but across the storm-white sea that separated Elephant Island from our landing place on South Georgia....One feels "the dearth of human words, the roughness of mortal speech" in trying to describe things intangible....[1]

That description by Shackleton of the mysterious fourth

member of the team admittedly limps in its attempt to identify the unaccountable member of the team.

Far more effective is T. S. Eliot's expression of Shackleton's fourth member in his poem, "What the Thunder Said," the fifth part of the *The Waste Land:*

> Who is the third who walks always beside you?
> When I count, there are only you and I together
> But when I look ahead up the white road
> There is always another one walking beside you
> Gliding wrapt in a brown mantle, hooded
> I do not know whether a man or a woman
> —But who is that one the other side of you?

In his notes on that passage, he observes that these lines "were stimulated by the account of one of the Antarctic expeditions (I forget which, but I think one of Shackleton's):...it was related that the party of explorers, at the extremity of their strength, had the constant delusion that there was *one more member* than could actually be counted."[2]

Eliot recognized the need to express mystery with tensive language. Anyone confronted with an occurrence that eludes reason needs to use appropriate language for that experience. Just as the experience surpasses human conventions of understanding, so must the language for that experience move beyond conventional descriptions.

Eliot maintained the tension between the third "who walks always beside you" and the two travelers that the observer can count.

Eliot's description of the unseen member does not attempt to be analytical, concrete, or clear. Rather he allows the numinous third member to be there, observed, but not counted. The tension in his language illumines the mystery of the fourth member of the team. The use of language to describe the tensive occurrence of the mysterious fourth member does not remove the numinous mist that befogged the three adventurers on their journey.

If Eliot had attempted to reduce the numinous event to careful description, he would have communicated that there was no mystery that the hikers encountered.

The comparison between Shackleton's and Eliot's language illustrates the thesis of this chapter: whoever attempts to express mystery needs to use tensive language. Shackleton attempted to use more analytical, concrete, and clear language to describe what was genuinely mysterious. His description is startling, but moves away from the mysterious dynamic that encountered him. Eliot on the other hand acknowledged that mystery by refusing to describe it analytically; instead he captured how the conscious experience of the three men in the team had strained away from their sense experience.

F. C. Happold's Encounter with Mystery

F. C. Happold cited his encounter with mystery on April 18, 1936, the evening before his son was born:

> It happened to me on the evening of 18 April 1936, the evening of the day before my son was born. My first child had been stillborn, and, as I lay in bed, I was very anxious about my wife and much disturbed in mind. And then a great peace came over me. I was conscious of a lovely, unexplainable pattern in the texture of things, a pattern of which everyone and everything was a part; and weaving the pattern was a Power; and that Power was what we faintly call Love. I realized that we are not lonely atoms in a cold, unfriendly, indifferent universe, but that each of us is linked up in a rhythm, of which we may be unconscious, and which we can never really know, but to which we can submit ourselves trustfully and unreservedly.[3]

Happold expressed the mystery of the presence of Love in a language which acknowledged the tension that was present in his encounter with the mystery. He added "each of us is linked up in a rhythm, of which we may be unconscious, and which we can never really know, but to which we can submit ourselves trustfully and unreservedly." He had experienced the mystery as encompassing each one of us, yet as beyond our consciousness. He could not adequately put his encounter with mystery into words, unless he articulated the tensive character of that encounter, in which the mystery encompasses each of us, yet is beyond our consciousness. It was not an occurrence that could be reduced to a clear and distinct idea.

Encountering Jesus Christ's Mystery

Similar to the mystery that Eliot's and Happold's expressions had articulated, the mystery of Jesus Christ's encounter with believers was expressed appropriately in the tensive dynamics of even the earliest Christian hymns. We can compare two that lean away from one another.

The first is the *Phos Hilaron* ("O Radiant Light"), which is an image of Christ Jesus.

O radiant Light, O son divine of God the Father's deathless face,
O image of the Light sublime that fills the heavenly dwelling place.

O Son of God, the source of life, Praise is your due by night and
     day.
Our happy lips must raise the strain of your esteemed and splendid
     name

Lord Jesus Christ, as daylight fades, as shine the lights of eventide,
We praise the Father with the Son, the Spirit blest, and with them one.

Here Christ Jesus was identified as "radiant Light," "Son divine of God," "Source of life," and as "Light sublime." It thus identifies him as more than human, as functioning in the manner of the Lord.

In contrast is the second of the earliest hymns, the *Bridle of Steeds Untamed,* which identifies Christ as one who could be grasped in more earthly terms:

> Bridle of steeds untamed
> Wing of flightless nestlings,
> Sure rudder of untried youth
> Shepherd of royal sheep.

Here Christ Jesus was identified as "Bridle," as "Wing of flightless nestlings," as "Sure rudder of untried youth," and as "Shepherd of royal sheep." The communities that used this early hymn considered Christ Jesus to be exalted above the conventional human individual, but identified him by means of images taken from human life. Thus the hymn praised Christ as one who could be identified within the envelope of life that surrounds the earth, not as one exalted to the level of the divine.

The early church communities preserved both of these hymns to Christ, because they reflected their faith that Christ was such a mystery that he had to be identified both with categories of the human and with those of the divine; those images strained against one another. This early, tensive confession of faith in Christ Jesus expresses the mystery of the Christ whom the church worshiped: he must belong exclusively neither to the earthly category nor to the heavenly category, but to both.

Yet there were and still are believers, such as Arius and modern-day agnostics, who insist that the identity of Christ Jesus must be reduced to clear and distinct categories. Arius had succinctly argued: God is eternal—there was when the Son was not, therefore the Son cannot be God. He presumed that faith was not mysterious, that the Son is not mystery, and that both faith and the Son are comprehensible. Arius and like-minded agnostics refuse to tolerate the tensive approach to the identity of Christ Jesus that the earliest hymns reveal. They do not recognize a mystery in Christ Jesus, but use reason as the standard by which to measure his identity.

On the other hand those who believe that mystery is needed in identifying Christ Jesus embrace the use of tensive language, as found in the tension between the early hymns *Phos Hilaron* and *Bridle of Steeds Untamed*. In the composite of those hymns Christ Jesus is identified as mystery who can be articulated only tensively.

The Task for Modern Believers

Present-day communities of believers might well heed those examples of the use of tensive language to express mystery. Just as the early communities, just as T. S. Eliot, and just as F. C. Happold recognized that they needed to use tensive language, so we might recognize that we too need to be tensive in our confession of Christ Jesus. He does not slip facilely into the category of a human being, nor even into that of the divine Lord. Rather he needs to be situated in a dialectic between those two. He eludes the rationalists' compulsion to reduce all occurrences, including enigmatic or mysterious individuals, to rationally comprehensible categories. Yet there continue to be people who insist that all occurrences, even enigmas, can be reduced to clear and distinct ideas. Such people refuse to acknowledge such occurrences as the believers' experience of Christ Jesus.

Nonetheless, there are believers who have been so encountered by Jesus Christ that they can identify him only in tensive language. They need to acknowledge that in their encounters with him there is an experience of the tension between the human and the divine.

Indeed Jesus was a human individual who had a historical existence in a specific geographical land within a specific historical age. He manifested in that place and age the kinds of needs, hopes, fears, and joys that reveal him to have been human. However those who were open to the dimension of faith-in-the-Spirit experienced him as an individual who continued to interact with them after his death. Paul of Tarsus was one of those.

Paul claimed not to have believed in Jesus as one who revealed God to humans.

> For you heard of my former way of life in Judaism, how I persecuted the church of God beyond measure and tried to destroy it, and progressed in Judaism beyond many of my contemporaries among my race, since I was even more a zealot for my ancestral traditions. But when [God], who from my mother's womb had set me apart and called me through his grace, was pleased to reveal his Son to me, so that I might proclaim him to the Gentiles, I did not immediately consult flesh and blood, nor did I go up to Jerusalem to those who were apostles before me; rather, I went into Arabia and then returned to Damascus. (Gal 1:13-17)

Paul says here that God led him to encounter God's "Son" some years after Jesus died. Paul acknowledges that this revelation was an encounter with a mystery that he could no longer resist. As a result of the mystery of his encounter with the Jesus who had died, Paul dedicated the rest of his life to serve Christ as Lord. No longer could Paul consider him to have been only human.

Individuals in the twentieth century continue to interact with Jesus. One whom Christ Jesus encountered is Mother Teresa of Calcutta. She explained her life as a response to her encounter with Christ Jesus in 1946:

> "It was," Mother Teresa told me, "on the tenth of September 1946, in the train to Darjeeling, the hill station in the Himalayas, that I heard the call of God."

Mother felt intensely that Jesus wanted her to serve him in the poorest of the poor, the uncared for, the slum dwellers, the abandoned, the homeless. Jesus invited her to serve him and follow him in actual poverty, material poverty, to practice a style of life that would make her similar to the needy in whom he was present, suffered, and loved.

Mother Mary Teresa answered, "Yes."

It was a flash of light on the road to Damascus, a meeting with Jesus.[4]

She understood her self-dedication to the thankless task of helping indigent people as her response to a call from her Lord, Christ Jesus, long after his death. He was still active in bidding her to so live and had even pledged to be there for her in the poor and deprived people to whom she would minister.

There are still many other believers who dedicate themselves to following Christ Jesus in bearing the cross and in serving humanity. For example, since the middle of this century the numbers of men and women who enter religious life have been plummeting—perhaps a consequence of the increasing secularization of Western culture. However as recently as thirty years previously, a great many men and women entered religious life as their response to a call from Christ Jesus, the Lord who interacted with them very long after his death. Many of those men and women continue to live vowed lives in response to that same Lord, whom they experience as continuing to summon them to follow him.

Conclusion

The contemporary believer cannot but respect the sophisticated expression of the earliest Christians' belief in

Christ Jesus. Even if no one community of early believers used all of the hymns cited in chapter 3, the church as an extended community preserved the bulk of the corpus of these hymns. One can presume therefore that the community of the early church understood that it believed in the *mystery of Christ*, not only in a Christ who could be grasped though simple categories.

Those who confess belief in Christ Jesus in the late twentieth century would do well to emulate the sophisticated belief of the earliest community of believers. Our faith would thus be much closer to the belief of the fathers of the Council of Chalcedon than if we simply confess without sophistication that Christ Jesus is God.

VIII. The Tensive Approach to Christ Jesus

Interpreting the meaning of Christ Jesus can only be adequately achieved by a tensive approach to the Lord. The early hymnmakers were quite modest when they approached the mystery of the identity of Christ Jesus. They were careful to acknowledge the seemingly contradictory dynamics within that mystery. They avoided any effort to sort out and reconcile contradictory assertions in the story of Jesus. So the early community confessed a belief in Christ Jesus in a way that was marked neither by clarity nor by use of distinctions. That tensive approach of the early communities in their ambivalent identification of Christ Jesus was passed on in the early hymns.

A few hundred years later the Fathers who gathered at the Council of Chalcedon were perceptive enough to recognize that the church's tradition of faith in Christ Jesus was tensive and ambivalent. They judged that they could integrate the many contradictory assertions about Jesus only if they used an approach that admitted that there remains in Christian faith a tensive relationship between Christ as the human Lord and Christ as the Son of God. They were also aware that they needed to be modest as they attempted to interpret the mystery of Christ; they did not presume an ability to render their interpretation of Jesus in logical terms that would reduce him from mystery to a comprehensible object that the human mind can understand.

Tensive, Dialectical Belief in Christ Jesus

The Fathers at Chalcedon were aware that the church community praised Christ as Son of God, as its Savior, as uniquely and intimately united with God.

However the Arian controversy made the Fathers conscious that, while Christ Jesus was the Son of God, his relationship with God could be addressed only by acknowledging that the identity of Christ as a human individual strained against his identity as the Son of God. The Arians had apparently succeeded in conditioning the majority of believers in the Mediterranean Basin to confess Christ not with a faith that suspends rational judgment, but with a judgment of clear logical analysis, which reduced Christ's relationship with the everlasting God to rational arguments. They had identified their confession as faith; yet, it was not faith, not a confession of that which lies beyond proof, but rather a confession of that which the followers of the Arians were able to demonstrate logically.

Those who made a true confession of faith, on the other hand, acknowledged that Jesus Christ exists in a tensive synthesis between Jesus as the Savior—the Son of God and the Promised One, sent from God to earth—and Jesus as human—the son of Mary. Their articulation of faith did not possess the gilded clarity and crispness that Arius had sought and had claimed to have achieved in their confession. It revealed more of a shading and ambiguity of a tensive relationship.

The Fathers of the Council of Chalcedon thus negotiated the Christological controversy by directing the community's belief in Christ Jesus away from the rational analysis of the Arians, away even from a spontaneous, communal response, toward a faithful use of the imagination to envision Christ. Ever since, Christian belief has confessed the imaginative, but complex Chalcedonian synthesis of the tensive doctrines about Christ Jesus.

Lingering Rational Approach to the Identity of Christ Jesus

The Arians did not accept the Council's decision, but continued to confess only an identity of him that their rational analysis would permit. They refused to commit themselves to Christ Jesus as accepted in imaginative belief.

Indeed after the Council of Chalcedon the fundamental weakness of the Arian position became manifest: there is evidence that an increasing number of the church community no longer aligned itself with the persuasive rationalism of the Arian argument, but accepted the tensive belief of the Chalcedonian approach. Evidence for that shift is found in the post-Chalcedonian hymns. Many hymns after 451 C.E., as chapter 3 demonstrates, suggest that the believing community were expressing a tensive belief in Christ. Their faith, manifest in their hymns, fulfilled Chalcedon's initial condition for faith in Christ; namely, that one faithfully confess Jesus' identity as the one who can be grasped only trustingly and imaginatively in the tension between his human and his divine identities.

Arius acknowledged only logical analysis as adequate for the confession of the doctrine about Christ. He did not make use of his imagination in identifying the relation between Christ Jesus and God. He judged that he had no need to be tensive in his belief, no need to move beyond rational labels. Yet he must have been aware of the tension between the various confessions of Christ, between the confession that he is the Son of God, that he is the Redeemer, and that he is the human Brother of all. He had to be aware that there were many bishops who opposed him precisely because they confessed their belief with a tension between the identity of Christ Jesus as human and as divine. Arius refused to admit that tension as a value in the confession of Christ. He continued to refuse to tolerate any ambiguity arising from the tension between the imaginative confession of Christ as human and Christ as divine. He insisted upon removing ambiguity in faith by removing belief in Christ from the range of the imagination and by reducing that belief to the demands of human logic.

Thus, while not only the earliest communities that preserved the earliest hymns, but also the bishops at Chalcedon admitted the need to use a tensive approach to the mystery of Christ, Arius chose to approach the identity of Christ with the methods of human reason.

There was for Arius nothing about Christ that placed him beyond the range of that which human reasoning can comprehend. Consequently Arius and those who had followed him—and those who continue to follow him—failed (and fail) to fulfill the criterion of the church's faith in Christ Jesus: a tensive belief.

That criterion is that which was manifest in the early hymns to Christ; namely, to confess belief in him as one who remains always within a tensive shade. In the early church, as in the present church, the believer needed and needs to confess not logical inferences about that which reason can grasp concerning Christ Jesus' identity. Rather, the believer must confess with imagination that Christ Jesus is one who can be grasped imaginatively as not only at the human pole—the individual who was born of Mary in Israel during the reign of Herod the Great, but also at the divine pole—the Promised One who is the Son of God and the One who acts as God's representative among humans.

Contemporary Dialectical Faith

The identity of Christ elaborated by the Council of Chalcedon creatively articulated the dialectical tension inherent in Jesus' identity. Christ Jesus is so mysterious an individual that the human mind cannot approach him univocally, as Arius insisted upon doing, but only equivocally or, better, tensively. It would have been for the fathers at Chalcedon as much of a violation of faith in Christ Jesus to have insisted that he was simply a man as to have insisted that he is God. The appropriate confession of faith in Christ Jesus was then and is now to insist that he is both a man and God, to insist that neither of those identities can be asserted without the other, and even to insist that neither of his identities modifies the other. Appropriate belief in Christ confessed then and confesses now the identity of Christ Jesus as divine—not divine by compromising his human identity, but rather by maintaining carefully that he is tensively both human and divine.

Clearly the bishops at Chalcedon insisted that belief in Christ Jesus is not a simple confession that he is God—not simply a confession of a statement about Christ asserted without nuances. On the contrary they fashioned a doctrine so complex that it requires believers to confess simultaneously not only Christ's identity as a human, but also his identity as the Son of God, whom God had sent to dwell among humans and to reveal God to them.

Since the Council of Chalcedon the church has formally expressed that tensive confession as one of the initial conditions for membership in the church community. That condition is also an initial step toward being humanly free: not that believers are free to choose their own goals or dictates of reason, but are free to choose to confess an *a*rational belief, a belief that follows not from reason, but from acknowledging that the presence and activity of God among humans is beyond the grasp of human reason, that God's presence in

Christ and among humans is outside of the categories for human experience.

Pope John XXIII imagined such human freedom in just that manner. He proposed that humans could achieve freedom tensively:

> Catholics need to believe that they will be saved. When they so increment their rational view worldview with a worldview of faith, they are free. When they so demonstrate that they function not only with the effort to understand, but also with the choice to believe, then they can be considered to be free human beings. That is the manner of living that the baptized adult is expected to adopt if one believes.[1]
>
> (trans. DPL)

This worldview of belief is critical for twentieth-century believers. The challenge of believing in the God of Christ Jesus is a summons to interpret experience not only with the human capacity to consider the data, to understand, and to judge, but also with the capacity to use one's imagination to accept that which has been grasped and expressed by others whom one trusts. The believer lives perhaps with unresolved tension, but nonetheless with the tensive dialectic between one's capacity of experiencing-understanding-and-judging and one's capacity of imaginatively trusting.

The tensive belief of hymns, even those used in contemporary Western, Christian worship, poses for modern believers a model of that tension.

Notes

I. Christology in Worship

1. Frankowski, "Early Christian Hymns," pp. 183-94.
2. Pollard, *Johannine Christology*, pp. 4-6.
3. Longenecker, *The Christology of Early Jewish Christianity*, pp. 59-62.

II. The Significance of Hymns: The Rule of Faith

1. Denzinger-Schoenmetzer, *Enchiridion Symbolorum*, Definitionum et Declarationum de rebus fidei et morum (Barcelona: Herder, 1963), # 246, 3792, 3828 .
2. Van Beeck, "Christian Faith and Theology," pp. 46-47.
3. Bengt Haegglund, "Bedeutung der 'regula fidei' als Grundlage theologischer Aussagen," *Studia Theologica* 12/ 1 (1958): pp. 1-44.
4. *The Church Teaches*, Documents of the Church in English Translation, Clarkson, Edwards, Kelly, Welch, eds. (St. Louis: Herder, 1965), # 80, pg. 34.
5. Athanasius, *Letter to Virgins* Johannes Quasten, *Patrology* (Westminster, Md.: Newman Press, 1950), 3, pp. 45-49.
6. *Griechischen Christlichen Shriftsteller der ersten drei Jahrhunderte, die* (Berlin: Akademie-Verlag, 1953), IV, 451-52.
7. Prosper of Aquitaine, *De vocatione omnium gentium*, Jacques-Paul Migne, ed., *Patrologiae Cursus Completus, Series Latina* 51, 664 C s. (Paris: J.-P. Migne, 1864), vol. 61, 664C s.

8. Jaroslav Pelikan, *The Christian Tradition: The Emergence of the Catholic Tradition* (Chicago: University of Chicago Press, 1971), pp. 172, 174, 189, 191, 200.

9. J. N. D. Kelly, *Early Christian Doctrines* (New York: Harper & Row, 1978), pp. 40-41.

10. Pelikan, *The Christian Tradition,* pp. 71-76.

11. Jaroslav Pelikan, *The Growth of Medieval Theology* (Chicago: University of Chicago Press, 1978), pp. 50-52.

12. Ibid., pp. 190, 194-200.

13. Thomas Aquinas, *Summa Theologica* (London: Burns Oates & Washbourne, 1942), II-II, Q. 1, a. 3, ad 3.

14. John Henry Newman, *On Consulting the Faithful* (New York: Sheed & Ward, 1961), pp. 53-106.

15. F. X. Connolly, "Newman, John Henry," *New Catholic Encyclopedia* (Washington, D.C.: McGraw Hill Book Co., 1967), vol. 10, pp. 413-14.

16. Clarkson, and others, *The Church Teaches,* pp. 29-32.

17. Denzinger-Schoenmetzer, # 3792.

18. Ibid., # 3828.

19. Norman Perrin, *Jesus and the Language of the Kingdom* (Philadelphia: Fortress Press, 1976), pp. 40-55.

20. Jean-Pierre Jossua, "Rule of Faith and Orthodoxy," translated by Lancelot Sheppard, in Edward Schillebeeckx, (ed.), *Dogma and Pluralism* (New York: Herder and Herder, 1970), pp. 56- 67.

21. Edward Schillebeeckx, *Revelation and Theology,* trans. N. D. Smith (London: Sheed and Ward, 1967), pp. 87-89.

22. James P. Mackey, *The Modern Theology of Tradition* (London: Darton, Longman, & Todd, 1962), pg. 149.

23. Yves Congar, *Tradition and Traditions* (New York: Macmillan, 1967), pg. 327.

24. Charles Hartshorne, *Divine Relativity* (New Haven: Yale University Press, 1948), pp. 16-17.

25. Rene Marle, "Hermeneutics and Scripture," translated by Matthew J. O'Connell; Rene Latourelle, and Gerald O'Collins eds., *Problems and Perspectives of Fundamental Theology* (New York: Paulist Press, 1982), pp. 69-86.

IV. The Pre-Nicaean Hymns Concerning Christ

1. Arius, translated by John Henry Newman, *The Arians of the Fourth Century*, pp. 215–16. Source for *Thalia: The Orations of St. Anthanasius against the Arians according to the Benedictine text*, I. 59, 62.

2. Samuel Duffield, *Latin Hymn-Writers and Their Hymns*, pg. 1.

3. Ibid., pg. 4.

4. Van Beeck, *God Encountered*, pp. 180–81.

5. Lionel Adley, *Hymns and the Christian "Myth,"* pp. 6, 208, n. 18.

6. W. Christ and M. Paranikas, eds. *Anthrologia Graeca Carminum Christianorum*, pp. xviii–xix.

7. F. Forrester Church and Terrence J. Mulry, *Earliest Christian Hymns*, pg. 29.

8. Charlesworth, *The Odes of Solomon*; this and all of the following Odes of Solomon are presented in English translation in Charlesworth's book on the Odes of Solomon.

9. Edmund Beck, *Die Theologie*, pg. 49.

10. Benedictines of Solesmes, *The Liber Usualis*, pp. 20–21.

11. Ibid., pp. 28–29.

12. Church and Mulry, *Earliest Christian Hymns*, pg. 203.

13. Duffield, *Latin Hymn-Writers and Their Hymns*, pg. 326.

14. Mulcahy, *Hymns of the Roman Breviary*, pg. 35.

15. Duffield, *Latin Hymn-Writers and Their Hymns*, pg. 50.

16. *Liber Usualis*, pg. 33.

17. Dom Matthew Britt, O.S.B., ed., *Hymns of the Breviary and Missal*, pg. 33.

18. Jesson, *Ambrosian Chant*, pp. 6, 16–26.

19. *Liber Usualis*, pp. 138–39.

20. Ibid., pg. 141.

21. Ibid., pg. 143.

22. Ibid., pp. 146–47.

23. Ibid., pp. 364–65.

24. Ibid., pg. 374.

25. Ibid., pp. 135–36.

26. Ibid., pp. 14–16.

27. Ibid., pp. 95-96.
28. Ibid., pg. 131.

V. The Early Church's Declarations about Christ in Its Hymns

1. Dickinson, *Music in the History of the Western Church*, pp. 1-34.
2. Nielen, *Earliest Christian Liturgy*, pp. 281-89.
3. Squire, *Church Music*, pp. 34-41.
4. Ibid.
5. Dickinson, *Music in the History of the Western Church*, pp. 35-69.
6. Timothy Gregory's *Vox Populi* argues that position as the thesis of the book.
7. *The Church Teaches*, pp. 1-2.

VI. The Development of the Controversies Leading Up to Chalcedon

1. Jaroslav Pelikan, *The Christian Tradition*, "The Catholic Tradition," pg. 195.
2. Ibid., pp. 273-74.
3. John Henry Cardinal Newman, *The Arians of the Fourth Century* (London: Longmans, Green, and Co., 1895), pp. 211-13. Pristine source: Theodoret; *Historia Ecclesiastica,* i. 4.
4. Leo Donald Davis, S.J., "Council of Nicaea I 325," *The First Seven Ecumenical Councils (325-787),* pg. 60.
5. Newman, *The Arians of the Fourth Century,* pp. 213-15.
6. Pelikan, *The Christian Tradition,* "The Catholic Tradition," pg. 161.
7. Ibid., pg. 173.
8. Ibid., pg. 188. Pristine source: Athanasius, *De synodis,* 16.
9. Ibid., pp. 177-78.
10. Ibid., pg. 230.
11. Ibid., pg. 231.

12. Ibid., pg. 251.

13. Ibid., pg. 252.

14. Ibid., pg. 247.

15. Ibid., pg. 249.

16. Ibid.

17. Ibid., pp. 258-59.

18. Ibid., pg. 264.

19. Ibid., pp. 265-66.

20. Cyril of Alexandria, "Cyril's Second Letter to Nestorius," Norris, *The Christological Controversy*, pp. 132-33.

21. Nestorius of Antioch, "Nestorius's Second Letter to Cyril," Norris, *The Christological Controversy*, pg. 136.

22. Pelikan, *The Christian Tradition*, "The Catholic Tradition," pg. 254.

23. Ibid., pg. 256.

VII. The Need for Tensive Dialectic to Express Mystery

1. Sir Ernest Henry Shackleton, *South*, pg. 209.

2. T. S. Eliot, "What the Thunder Said," and notes, *The Complete Poems and Plays*, pp. 48, 54.

3. F. C Happold, *Religious Faith and Twentieth-Century Man*, pg. 15.

4. Edward Le Joly, S.J., *Mother Teresa of Calcutta*, "The Call," pp. 9-10.

VIII. The Tensive Approach to Christ Jesus

1. K 2aa in Denzinger-Schoenmetzer, pg. 867.

Bibliography

Articles

Baroffio, Giacomo Bonifacto. "Ambrosian Rite." In *The New Grove Dictionary of Music and Musicians*, ed. Stanley Sadie, vol. 1, pp. 314–20. London: Macmillan, 1980.

Beasley-Murray, Paul. "Colossians 1:15–20: An Early Christian Hymn Celebrating the Lordship of Christ." *Pauline Studies*, Donald A. Hagner and Murray J. Harris, pp. 169–83. Grand Rapids Mich.: Eerdmans, 1980.

Beeck, Frans Jozef van, S.J. "Christian Faith and Theology in Encounter with Non-Christians: Profession? Protestation? Self-Maintenance? Abandon?" *Theological Studies* 55 (1994): pp. 46–65.

Connolly, F. X. "Newman, John Henry." *New Catholic Encyclopedia*, vol. 10, pp. 413–14. Washington, D.C.: McGraw-Hill, 1967.

"Didache" or "Teaching of the Apostles." *The Fathers of the Church— The Apostolic Fathers*, trans. F. X. Glimm, Joseph Marique, and Gerald Walsh, pp. 171–84. New York: CIMA Publishing, 1947.

Farmer, William R. "Galatians and the Second-Century Development of the *Regula Fidei*." *Second Century* 4, no. 3 (Fall 1985): pp. 143–70.

Frankowski, Janusz. "Early Christian Hymns Recorded in the New Testament, a Reconsideration of the Question in the Light of Heb 1:3." *Biblische Zeitschrift* 27, no. 2 (1983): pp. 183–94. Paderborn: Verlag Ferdinand Schoeningh, 1983.

Haegglund, Bengt. "Die Bedeutung der 'Regula Fide' als Grundlage theologischer Aussagen." *Studia Theologica* 12, no. 1 (1958): pp. 1-44.

Hanson, Richard P. C. "The Church and Tradition in the Pre-Nicene Fathers." *Scottish Journal of Theology* 12 (1959): pp. 21-31.

Jossua, Jean-Pierre. "Rule of Faith and Orthodoxy." *Dogma and Pluralism,* ed. Edward Schillebeeckx, trans. Lancelot Sheppard, pp. 56-67. New York: Herder and Herder, 1970.

Marle, Rene. "Hermeneutics and Scripture." In *Problems and Perspectives of Fundamental Theology,* edited by Rene Latourelle, and Gerald O'Collins, trans. Matthew J. O'Connell, pp. 69-86. Ramsey, N.J.: Paulist Press, 1982.

Newman, John Henry Cardinal. *The Arians of the Fourth Century.* London: Longmans, Green, 1895.

Outler, Albert C. "Origen and the Regula Fidei." *Second Century* 4, no. 3 (1985): pp. 133-41.

Prosper of Aquitaine. "De Vocatione Omnium Gentium." In *Patrologiae Cursus Completus; Series Latina* 61 (664C s). Paris: 1864.

Robeck, Cecil M. "Canon, *Regula Fidei,* and Continuing Revelation in the Early Church." In *Church, Word, and Spirit*: Historical and Theological Essays, by James E. Bradley and edited by Richard Muller. (Grand Rapids, Mich): Eerdmans, 1987, pp. 65-91.

Rodd, Cyril. "Salvation Proclaimed—Colossians 2:8-15." *The Expository Times* 94 (Nov. 1982): pp. 36-41.

"The Shepherd of Hermas." *The Fathers of the Church—The Apostolic Fathers*, trans. F. X. Glimm, Joseph Marique, and Gerald Walsh, pp. 233-350. New York: CIMA Publishing, 1947.

Vawter, Bruce, C.M. "The Colossians Hymn and the Principle of Redaction." *Catholic Biblical Quarterly* 33 (1971): pp. 62-81.

Books

Adley, Lionel. *Hymns and the Christian "Myth."* Vancouver: University of British Columbia Press, 1986.

Allmen, J. J. von. *Worship: Its Theology and Practice.* New York: Oxford University Press, 1965.

Athanasius of Alexandria. *Orations of S. Athanasius Against the Arians*. London: Griffith Farran Okeden & Welsh, n.d.

Beck, Edmund, O.S.B. *Die Theologie des Hl. Ephraem*. Rome: Vatican Library, 1949.

Beeck, Frans Jozef van, S.J. *Catholic Identity After Vatican II*. Chicago: Loyola University Press, 1985.

———. *Christ Proclaimed*. Mahwah, N.J.: Paulist Press, 1979.

———. *God Encountered*. Vol. I: Understanding the Christian Faith. San Francisco: Harper & Row, 1988.

———. *Loving the Torah More than God?* Chicago: Loyola University Press, 1989.

Benedictines of Solesmes, eds. *The Liber Usualis*. New York: J. Fischer & Bro., 1938.

Bouillard, Henri. *Blondel and Christianity*, translated by James M. Somerville. Washington, D.C.: Corpus Books, 1969.

Bradley, James E. and Richard A. Muller, eds. *Church, Word, and Spirit,* Historical and Theological Essays. Grand Rapids, Mich.: Eerdmans, 1987.

Britt, Dom Matthew, O.S.B., ed. *The Hymns of the Breviary and Missal*. New York: Benzinger Brothers, 1948.

Brown, Raymond E. *The Community of the Beloved Disciple*. Mahwah, N.J.: Paulist Press, 1979.

Brown, Raymond, Joseph Fitzmyer, and Roland Murphy, eds. *The New Jerome Biblical Commentary*. Englewood Cliffs, N.J.: Prentice-Hall, 1990.

Charlesworth, James Hamilton, trans. and ed. *The Odes of Solomon*. Oxford: Clarendon Press, 1973.

Christ, W. and M. Paranikas, eds. *Anthologia Graeca Carminum Christianorum*. Stuttgart: B. G. Teubner Verlag, 1963.

Church, F. Forrester and Terrence J. Mulry, eds. *Earliest Christian Hymns*. New York: Macmillan, 1988.

The Church Teaches, Documents of the Church in English Translation. Clarkson, Edwards, Kelly, Welch, eds. St. Louis: Herder, 1965.

Congar, Yves. *Tradition and Traditions*. New York: Macmillan, 1967.

Cullmann, Oscar. *Early Christian Worship*. London: SCM Press, 1953.

Davis, Leo Donald, S.J. *The First Seven Ecumenical Councils (325-787)*. Collegeville, Minn.: Liturgical Press, 1990.

Denzinger-Schoenmetzer. *Enchiridion Symbolorum*, Definitionum et Declarationum de rebus fidei et morum. Barcelona: Herder, 1963.

Dickson, Edward. *Music in the History of the Western Church*. New York: Charles Scribner's Sons, 1902.

Donahoe, Daniel Joseph. *Early Christian Hymns*: Translations of the Verses of the Most Notable Latin Writers of the Early and Middle Ages. New York: Grafton Press Publishers Publishers, 1908.

Dwyer, John C. *Son of Man & Son of God*: A New Language for Faith. Ramsey, N.J.: Paulist Press, 1983.

Eliot, T. S., *The Complete Poems and Plays, 1909-1950*. New York: Harcourt Brace, 1971.

Fackenheim, Emil L. *The Religious Dimension in Hegel's Thought*. Bloomington: Indiana University Press, 1967.

Fichte, Johann Gottlieb. *Science of Knowledge (Wissenschaftslehre)*. Edited and translated by Peter Heath and John Lachs. New York: Appleton-Century-Crofts, 1970.

Gregg, Robert C. and Dennis E. Groh, *Early Arianism—A View of Salvation*. Philadelphia: Fortress Press, 1981.

Gregory, Timothy E. *Vox Populi*: Popular Opinion and Violence in the Religious Controversies of the Fifth Century A.D. Columbus: Ohio State University Press, 1979.

Griechische Christlichen Shriftsteller der ersten drei Jahrhunderte, die. Berlin: Akademie-Verlag, 1953.

Grillmeier, Alois. *Jesus Christus im Glauben der Kirche*. Band 1: Von der Apostolischen Zeit bus zum Konzil von Chalcedon (451). Freiburg: Herder, 1979.

Grout, Donald Jay. *A History of Western Music*. Revised edition. New York: W. W. Norton, 1973.

Hagner, Donald A. and Murray J. Harris, eds. *Pauline Studies*: Essays presented to Professor E. F. Bruce on His 70th Birthday. Grand Rapids, Mich.: Wm. B. Eerdmans, 1980.

Hahn, Ferdinand. *The Worship of the Early Church*. Philadelphia: Fortress Press, 1973.

Happold, F. C. *Religious Faith and Twentieth-Century Man*. Baltimore: Penguin Books, 1966.

Harnack, Adolph von. *History of Dogma*. Translated from the third German edition by Neil Buchanan. Boston: Roberts Brothers, 1897.

Hartshorne, Charles. *Divine Relativity*. New Haven: Yale University Press, 1948.

Hegel, Georg Wilhelm Friedrich. *The Philosophy of History*. Translated by J. Sibree. New York: Willey Book Co., 1900.

Holladay, Carl R. *Theios Aner in Hellenistic Judaism*: A Critique of the Use of this Category in New Testament Christology. Missoula, Mont.: Scholars Press for the Society of Biblical Literature, 1977.

Jesson, Roy H. *Ambrosian Chant: The Music of the Mass*. Ann Arbor, Mich.: University Microfilms International, 1955.

Johnson, Luke Timothy. *The Writings of the New Testament: An Interpretation*. Philadelphia: Fortress Press, 1986.

Julian, John, D.D. *A Dictionary of Hymnology*: Setting Forth the Origin and History of Christian Hymns of All Ages and Nations. London: John Murray, 1907.

Kautsky, Karl. *Der Ursprung des Christentums*. Hannover: Verlag J. H. W. Dietz Nachf., 1968.

Kroll, Josef. *Die Christliche Hymnodik bus zu Klemens von Alexandreia*. Darmstadt: Wissenschaftliche Buchgesellschaft, 1921.

Lang, Paul Henry. *Music in Western Civilization*. New York: W. W. Norton, 1969.

Lattey, Father C., S.J. *The Pre-Nicene Church*. London: Burns Oates & Washbourne Ltd., 1935.

LeJoly, Edward, S.J. *Mother Teresa of Calcutta, a Biography*. San Francisco: Harper & Row, 1977.

Longenecker, Richard N. *The Christology of Early Jewish Christianity*. Naperville, Ill.: Alec R. Allenson, 1970.

Mackey, James P. *The Modern Theology of Tradition*. London: Darton, Longman, & Todd, 1962.

Milet, Jean. *God or Christ?* The Excesses of Christocentricity. Trans. John Bowden. New York: Crossroad, 1981.

Mulcahy, Rev. Cornelius Canon. *Hymns of the Roman Breviary and Missal*. Dublin: Browne and Nolan, Ltd., 1938.

Neale, Rev. J. M., ed. and transl. *Hymns of the Eastern Church.* London: J. T. Hayes, 1862.

Newman, John Henry Cardinal. *The Arians of the Fourth Century.* London: Longmans, Green, and Co., 1895.

_____. *On Consulting the Faithful in Matters of Doctrine.* New York: Sheed & Ward, 1961.

Nielen, Josef Maria. *The Earliest Christian Liturgy.* St. Louis, Mo.: B. Herder, 1941.

Norris, Richard A., Jr., trans. and ed. *The Christological Controversy.* Philadelphia: Fortress Press, 1980.

Orations of St. Athanasius against the Arians according to the Benedictine Text. Oxford: Clarendon Press, 1873.

Pelikan, Jaroslav. *The Christian Tradition: The Emergence of the Catholic Tradition (100-600).* Chicago: University of Chicago Press, 1971.

_____. *The Christian Tradition: The Growth of Medieval Theology (600-1300).* Chicago: University of Chicago Press, 1978.

Perrin, Norman. *Jesus and the Language of the Kingdom:* Symbol and Metaphor in New Testament Interpretation. Philadelphia: Fortress Press, 1976.

_____. *The New Testament: An Introduction.* New York: Harcourt Brace Jovanovich, 1974.

Pollard, T. E. *Johannine Christology and the Early Church.* Cambridge: Cambridge University Press, 1970.

Prudentius, *The Fathers of the Church—The Poems of Prudentius, vv. 1 and 2.* Translated by Sr. M. Clement Egan. Washington, D.C.: Catholic University of America Press, 1962.

Quasten, Johannes. *Patrology.* Westminster, Md.: Newman Press, 1950.

Raby, F. J. E. *A History of Christian-Latin Poetry:* From the Beginnings to the Close of the Middle Ages. Oxford: Clarendon Press, 1953.

Schaff, Philip. *History of the Christian Church.* Vol. 2: Ante-Nicene Christianity—A.D. 100-325. Grand Rapids, Mich.: Wm B. Eerdmans, 1950.

Schillebeeckx, Edward. *Revelation and Theology.* Trans. N. D. Smith. London: Sheed & Ward, 1967.

Shackleton, Sir Ernest Henry, *South: The Story of Shackleton's Last*

Expedition, 1914-1917. Ed. Peter King London: Century Pub., 1991, pg. 209.

Squire, Russel N. *Church Music: Musical Hymnological Development in Western Christianity.* St. Louis, Mo.: Bethany Press, 1962.

Thomas Aquinas, St. *Summa Theologica.* London: Burns Oates & Washbourne, 1942.

Wagner, Johannes, ed. Concilium Series. *The Church and the Liturgy.* Glen Rock, N.J.: Paulist Press, 1965.

Walpole, A. S. and A. J. Mason, eds. *Early Latin Hymns.* London: Cambridge University Press, 1922.

Index